Eulogies

Eulogies

Amiri Baraka

MARSILIO PUBLISHERS

NEW YORK

Some of these poems and essays first appeared in the following
publications:

African American Review
Amsterdam News
Antaeus
Black Nation
City Sun

Jihad
New American Writing
Perspectives
Stepping Stones
Sulfur

Amiri Baraka Reader
Black Magic
Selected Poetry

"Ghost Poem #1" and "Poppa Stoppa Speaks from the Grave" by Larry
Neal is reprinted by permission of Evelyn Neal

Selection from "The Book of Genesis According to Saint Miguelito" by
Miguel Pinero is reprinted by permission of Miguel Algarin

Selection from *Evidence of Things Not Seen* by James Baldwin is reprinted
by permission of the James Baldwin Estate. Copyright ©1985, 1995

MARSILIO PUBLISHERS
853 BROADWAY, NEW YORK, NY 10003

DISTRIBUTED IN THE U.S.A. BY
CONSORTIUM BOOK SALES & DISTRIBUTION
1045 WESTGATE DRIVE, SAINT PAUL, MN 55114-1065

ISBN 1-568886-007-2

For my wife, Amina,
who has known and loved these people as well.

Foreword

This book provides a summing up of a period of history. You don't want to consider it until you see it, but a large part of this whole generation that we thought would be young forever is not here any more. Recently I realized, Jesus, there are a lot of us gone, and I'm getting older too.

As a writer who came of age with a lot of these people, I was naturally often asked by the families to say something at the memorial services. It means a lot to me to have been asked and to have had these "opportunities". These are my maximum cultural/political heroes and my extended community and human family. These are the ones I grew up with, loved, and was/am influenced by. They are the fighters, the advanced, the artists, the intellectuals—people discontent with things as they are. Not all of them are well known, but they all represent a developed and advanced way of living in the world.

Most of these pieces were delivered in churches in Newark, New York City, and Philly. For me, writing a eulogy is very much part of a writer's central purpose, which is not supposed to be serving as a spontaneous reflector of one's self, but as an investigator of a useful shared vision.

In describing these lives, I was trying to provide a record of their contributions, their sensibilities, their artistic intentions or their ideals, but also the world they lived in. In offering this collection, I want to help pass on what needs to live on not just in the archive but on the sidewalk of Afro-America itself.

—A.B.

TABLE OF CONTENTS

Eulogies

Malcolm X (1925-1965)

A Poem for Black Hearts

For Malcolm's eyes, when they broke
the face of some dumb white man, For
Malcolm's hands raised to bless us
all black and strong in his image
of ourselves, For Malcolm's words
fire darts, the victor's tireless
thrusts, words hung above the world
change as it may, he said it, and
for this he was killed, for saying,
and feeling, and being/ change, all
collected hot in his heart, For Malcolm's
heart, raising us above our filthy cities,
for his stride, and his beat, and his address
to the grey monsters of the world, For Malcolm's
pleas for your dignity, black man, for your life,
black man, for the filling of your minds
with righteousness, For all of him dead and
gone and vanished from us, and all of him which
clings to our speech black god of our time.
For all of him, and all of yourself, look up,
black man, quit stuttering and shuffling, look up,
black man, quit whining and stooping, for all of him,
For Great Malcolm a prince of the earth, let nothing in us rest
until we avenge ourselves for his death, stupid animals
that killed him, let us never breathe a pure breath if
we fail, and white men call us faggots till the end of
the earth.

John Coltrane (1926-1967)

I Love Music

"I want to be a force for real good.
In other words, I know that there are bad forces,
forces that bring suffering to others and misery to the world,
but I want to be the opposite
force. I want to be the force which is truly
for good."

Trane

Trane

Trane sd,

A force for real good, Trane. in other words. Feb '67
By july he was dead.
By july. He said in other words
he wanted to be the opposite
but by July he was dead, but he is, offering
expression a love supreme, afroblue in me singing
it all because of him
can be
screaming beauty
can be
afroblue can be
you leave me breathless
can be
      alabama
               I want to talk about you
                             my favorite things
                                         like sonny

can be

life itself, fire can be, heart explosion, soul explosion, brain explosion
can be. can be. can be. aggeeewheeeuheageeee. aeeegeheooouaaaa
deep deep deep
expression deep, can be
capitalism dying, can be
all, see, aggggeeeeoooo. aggrggrrgeeeoouuuu. full full full can be
empty too.
nightfall by water
round moon over slums
shit in a dropper
soft face under fingertips trembling
can be

can be
can be, trane, can be, trane, because of trane, because
world world world world
can be
sean o' casey in ireland
can be, lu hsun in china
can be,
        brecht wailing
                gorky   riffing
                        langston hughes steaming
                                                    can be
                                                    trane
                                                    bird's main man
                                                    can be

            big maybelle can be
        workout workout workout
                            expression
                            Ogunde
                            afroblue can be
all of it meaning, essence, revelation, everything together, wailing in
unison
                        a terrible
wholeness

3

Amilcar Cabral (1924-1973)

Afrikan Revolution

(Conakry, Guinea, February 4, 1973 after Amilcar Cabral's funeral)

Afrikan People all over the world
Suffering from white domination
Afrikan People all over the world
Trying to liberate their Afrikan nation(s)
Afrikan People all over the world
Under the yoke, the gun, the hammer, the lash
Afrikan People all over the world
being killed & stifled melted down for the white boys cash
Afrikan People all over the world
   conscious, unconscious, struggling, sleeping
resisting, tomming, killing the enemy killing each other
Being hurt, surviving, understanding, held in ignorance
Bursting out of chains, lying for Nixon, drowning colonialists
Being shot down in the street
Afrikan People everywhere
Afrikan People all over the world
Evolving because of & in spite of ourselves
Afrikan People all over the world, trying to make Revolution
The world must be changed, split open & changed
All poverty sickness ignorance racism must be eradicated
Whoever pushes these plagues, them also must be eradicated
All capitalists, racists, liars, Imperialists, All who can not change
they also must be eradicated, their life style, philosophies
habits, flunkies, pleasures, wiped out—eliminated
The world must be changed, split open & changed
Transformed, turned upside down
No more Poverty!
No more dirty ragged black people, cept from hard work
   to beautify + energize a world we help create

4

Death to Backward Powers
Death to Bad Dancers
    No more trash piled up in the streets
    No more wind in the bedroom
No more Europeans in penthouses & colored people in tents
    with no houses
Death to disease & carriers of disease
All disease must be cured!
"Individuals" who love disease must be reeducated
If they resist world unity and the progress of all races
Kill them. Don't hesitate! Kill them. They are the Plague
No more filthy places for us to live and be uneducated
No more aimless black children with nothing to do, but die
Death to the creators of unemployment
What do they do for a living? They are thieves
Jail them! Nixon is a sick thief why does he
remain alive? who is in charge of killing him?
Why is it Cabral, Lumumba, Nkrumah, Moumie,
Malcolm, Dr. King, Mondlane, Mark Essex, all can
be killed by criminals, & the criminals are not
hung from bridges? No more unfair societies!
We are for world progress. Be conscious of your
life! We need food. We need homes; good
housing—not shacks. Let only people who want to
live in roach gyms live in roach gyms
We do not want to live with roaches. Let
Nixon live with roaches if he wants to. He
is closer to a roach. What is the difference
between Nixon and a roach?
Death to bad housing
Death to no work
We need work. We need education so
we can build houses and create work for
ourselves. All over the world we Afrikans
need to make progress. Why do Europeans
Why do white people why do ignorant
people of our own race obstruct us?

STOP OBSTRUCTING US EUROPEANS!
STOP OBSTRUCTING US IGNORANT PEOPLE OF
    OUR OWN RACE
        Niggers, NeoColonized Amos + Andies
        Everywhere in the Afrikan World.
No more traitors! Death to traitors
        Dope Pushers should be killed
        Niggers who inform on Revolutionary Movements
        Should be killed
        Assassins masquerading as heroes
        Butlers masquerading as presidents of
            Afrikan, & Asian & South Amerikan
            Nations. They have made them Dough-Nations
So the white boy can make his bread.
        Leaders who want dialogue with South Afrika
        Leaders who want to box in South Afrika
        Leaders who want to sing in South Afrika
        Leaders who want to observe South Afrika
These are not Leaders but Pleaders and
they should be beaten till their yoke and
their white are stiff & exposed
No more useless pain
We must refuse to be sold out by anyone
The world can be changed, we do not have to lick
    the pavements
All over the world the world can be changed
No more stupid ugliness everywhere
Death to the vultures of primitive disease +
    ignorance, America must change or be
    destroyed. Europe must change or be
    destroyed. Capitalism must be destroyed.
    Imperialism will die. Empty headed
    mummified niggers who support white
    rule over black people will be killed too.
    Dope peddlers, Pimps, Teachers who teach
    Europe's lies, Doctors who love money more
    than people, muggers, pretenders of revolution,

Sterile intellectuals, Soul singers who
Sold their soul to the soulless—live people who live
their lives for the dead—all change or die!
The world revolution cannot be stopped. Understand the
new criteria of life or forfeit what little life you have.
We will not be poor any longer
We will not be dirty, or ashamed of ourselves
    Racists, Capitalists, Imperialists, Sick People
    Fascists, white rulers of Black,
    Lovers of disease, change or die
    Oppressed People of the world change
    or die
    Afrikan People, all over the world Rise
    & Shine
    Shine
    Shine

Afrikan People all over the world, the future is ours
We will create on our feet not our knees
It is a future of Great works and Freedom
But we can not crawl through life drunk &
unconscious we cannot dance through life
or read the NYTimes through life, or wear vests
all of our life give our lives to parties, & work with no
reason but life in a prison of white domination,
Be conscious. Black People
    Negroes
    Colored People
    Afro Americans Be
        CONSCIOUS
You know you can run your own life
You can have all the money & food & good life
you need
    Be conscious
    meet once a week
Meet once a week. Talk about how to get
    more money, how to get educated, how

to have scientists for children rather than
junkies. How to kill the roaches. How to
stop the toilet from stinking. How to get a
better job. Once a week. Start NOW.
How to dress better. How to read.
How to live longer. How to be respected.
Meet once a week. Once a week.

All over the world. We need to meet once a
    week. All over the world Afrikans, Soul
    Brothers Good Sisters we need to meet.
How to live longer be healthier build houses
run cities understand life be happier
Need to meet once a week
OK All over the world
Once a week
All over the world Afrikans
Sweet Beautiful Afrikans
NewArk Afrikans (Niggers too)
Harlem Afrikans (or Spooks)
Ghana Afrikans (Bloods)
Los Angeles Afrikans (Brothers)
Afrikan Afrikans (Ndugu)
West Indian Afrikans (Hey man)
South American Afrikans (Hermano!)
Francophone Afrikans (Monsieur)
Anglophone Afrikans (Mister Man)
Anywhere Afrikans
Afrikans Afrikans Afrikans
People
Afrikans Afrikans Afrikans
Watu Wazuri
Afrikans all over the world
Moving to the new way
A world of Good people is coming!
We gonna help make that world
We gonna help eliminate the negative

accentuate the positive
yellow folks brown folks red
folks will too
they hurting
I can't speak for white folks, they'll
speak for themselves
But the rest of us, Everybody Everybody
Everybody, let us first deal with us
Afrikans
All over the world, Yes, Everywhere Everywhere
Everywhere, we are Afrikans
& going to make change
Change or die
Afrikans
Change or die
to the Whole world too
we are Afrikans
Love is our passport to the perfectability of humanity
Work & Study
Struggle & Victory
some way!!

1983

Anna Russ (1885-1962) and Fanny Jones (1885-1976)

A Poem for Anna Russ and Fanny Jones

An old story the world old now for us who was once a young
    stormy buck railing railing
even the tone sounding inside for the change of things that we
    never knew, was heavy, it
shimmered colors nobody ever seen. Yet it had to be run down
    finally, it had to control
and discipline itself, it had to make absolute sense, and pt out
    clearly what it meant.
Who were its enemies, this consciousness is what I mean, this
    feeling abt life, reality,
is a people's, is a nation's, is a link tho, to a billion people every
    where trying to live
and understand. Your skin scraped off so the moonlight stings,
    so the swish of bird's wings
brings a message to the brain. Where the perception mashes
    continuous a message from the
world. A link with the billions. This is the world. We are in it.
    We can live and survive
at a higher level. We can advance all life to higher ground. And
    the quiet grandmothers died
and went to "heaven" could take note of the same feeling cause
    that's what they had to mean
if the metaphysical cloak their times had draped on their world
    was translated. There is a
better life, but it's in the world, in the lives of the people, we just
have to struggle, we
just have to care and take care and study, we just have to fight
    some more people's wars.
That wd be the hymn underneath, we will meet again on higher
    ground. That all society will
be raised to higher ground, a more advanced life. And that feeling

has burned in me since
the dawn of my life. That all of us cd meet on higher ground.
    And now it has to come out·
very straight and clear. That this is not possible without violence
    and revolution, that
there is no higher ground possible without the destruction of real
    evil which is capitalism
and the rule of the rich. That the rule of the tiny minority must
    be crushed by the billions
and this is the clear message that has to come out, that cannot
    be hidden with lyricality
and mysticism or vagueness and romanticism. It has to be said,
    and having said it, the monsters
conspire to kill those who dare make it plain. They huddle and
plot our repression and pain. But
just like the old stories grandmama, that aint no big thing, we
    learned how evil wd act in
Sunday School, and how the people, the righteous, wd always win!

1976

Al Ryan (1931-1980)

Al Ryan

Al & me and a whole lot of Black People go back to the '60s. That was our explosion into consciousness. And that's where Al & I hooked up. Amidst the forming of new organizations, new commitments, new clarity, I met him in an L.A. that just came awake screaming in Watts, an L.A. that turned African and bathed in Swahili melody. And we talked and laughed and plotted together at the various Black Power Conferences, he was a regular. One of the desirers, on the serious side, of Black Power.

From the first time I met Al the overwhelming quality he communicated to me was sensitivity. A sensitive thoughtful brother was how you felt about him. There was a deepness to Al, a quality of depth that was always reassuring. Because no matter what we say we want or who we say we are, what we really are is always obvious to the close observer.

Al had studied to be an attorney, a lawyer. But that meant something else to him, finally. What those studies did for Al connected him to us more urgently than it prepared him to define himself according to the criteria of the oppressively powerful. Al wanted to do something, he wanted us all to do something, so that we could be more than we were.

Al & I got closer in the '70s with the historic gathering in Atlanta, the Congress of African People. We were together with thousands of other Black people talking about Unity and Liberation. Those things were close to Al, which is why we always remained close friends. And as the movement thrust forward in its various twists and turns, I always counted on Al as the West Coast man. Al would know. Al could find out. Al would be there. We were all Revolutionary Optimists in those days, in our better moments, in our worse moments we were just Romantics and

Idealists. But the rightness of our cause gave us, no matter, an unassailable energy, an admirable persistence!

In Gary, Indiana, in 1972, 8,000 Black People came together to roar our solidarity, our willingness to struggle. And though we did suffer from some of the same lack of science and thorough analysis, we did possess the burning spirit without which, armed even with the best of theories, we could not win!

Al was the West Coast man, the connector, the vector. He sat in endless meetings with us, as we tried and struggled to build the Black United Front that we still must build if we are ever to be free! Al traveled back and forth, spent sleepless nights and weary talk-heavy days. Arguments, screamings, disappointments, fist-fights, and laughter and brotherhood too, all these were part of that master course in the Black Liberation Movement.

You see, that is one of the terrible things about Al's leaving us, he'd been there, he'd seen and understood things, he'd walked that twisted jumbled road with those of us who actually took up the yoke of Black People's struggle. And so we have lost not only a sensitive brother but an experienced struggler here in Babylon. Because now Al was a teacher, a guide. And I'm sure many people knew that. He wasn't just talking; he'd been to the mountain and knew what still has to be done, yes, Al knew what still has to be done.

And when the movement reached an impasse in the mid—'70s, when some of us went left and others went right, Al and I talked and he questioned because he wanted to understand, to know what was happening, where were we, where are we going. And we came back together on still a higher level, after our sojourn in the school of practice and struggle of the '60s and early '70s, we had learned and were prepared, had begun, to start doing again, armed with information and science gained in that school of hard knocks.

Whenever I came west I talked to Al. Slept in his house, played with his kids. He rented a place in Venice, California for my family and I to stay a week or so one summer. Most of what I know about Los Angeles, Al Ryan passed it on. Frequently, he organized poetry readings and speaking engagements in this town for me. And just recently, when I came out here to speak in L.A. and San

Francisco, I met Al again after the speech, we went to a bar, and drank beer and talked. We were summing things up, what had happened, what was happening, what needed to happen. And I remember, as we started to split, we stood in a parking lot, still talking, still analyzing and plotting, still caught up in the dynamic of unity and liberation, still very intense in our different ways, about Black Self-Determination. We hugged each other, like we always did, when we met or when we booked. We waved as I got in another car headed for the airport. I thought I've got to send Al some things I was making notes on, some things we'd talked about. "Hey, Man, take care of yourself," was the way Al put it. "Hey, you take care of yrself," I shouted back. So quickly our lives pass by us, let us more consciously use them. Al was my main man.

1980

Art Williams (1922-1980)

Art

I knew Art Williams since we were both real young. Me a little younger. I knew Art and his brother, Cliff, who was a terrible dude with a pencil or pen, a dynamite draughtsman even then. Another brother.

And we ran into each other, going our various ways. Heard, I imagine, about what each other was doing. You know how that is. An image here, another there, years later.

When I left Newark going to Howard and then continued out of school into the Error Farce and then to New York, trying to find out where the big time intellectuals hung (& that, in itself, is a tale). After a while, like in most cases I had lost track of all of the Williamses, to be sure.

When I came back to Newark at the beginning of 1966, the first person I hear about, from wherever is Art. I had forgotten he was a musician, a bass player. But when I got back and finally got a place to live, I rented this old house on Stirling St. and knocked down the walls on the 1st floor to make a theater, Black Arts style. It turned out, ironically enough, that I was living just a few steps, a couple of short blocks from Art's spot.

It was called The Cellar and it was just that, a cellar in an industrial building. A flight down, and when you walked in there usually, one of those nights, the music would reach up at you from those depths and glide you in like one of those airplanes floating in via the glide path.

The Cellar was, during the late '60s, the place, if you dug the heavy sounds, the real "avant," the new hip. Art turned the place into an intimate art room, heavy on the music, but also many poetry readings. I read there. Yusef Rahman, John Sinclair, and a bunch of other people.

Art was a member of the original Jazz Arts Society ("The Loft") in which my wife Amina, then Sylvia Robinson, was a catalyzing force. Rahman Herbie Morgan, Jimmy Anderson, Tom White, were some other members. It was an important creation in continuing to stimulate and develop the progressive and innovative cultural revolution emerging in Newark in the late '60s, Part of the rising dynamic for change that characterizes that whole period, particularly as it relates to the Afro-American people's continuous historical struggle for Self-Determination.

You could not wait for people who hated you to create institutions for you. Except jails. The Black Arts movement had galvanized Afro-American artists across the country to express that the Art and the Culture of Black People must be developed by them, as an act of Self-Determination, as Malcolm X said, Self-Respect and Self-Defense.

Elijah Muhammad and The Nation of Islam were saying, as they had for years, even before Malcolm, "Do For Self." You want to hear the music play it for yourself and make money create an institution to do it in.

And this theme has relentlessly been expressed at every political upsurge the Afro-American people have ever made. Garvey and DuBois had said this even before Elijah Muhammad. And many others. "Do For Self!"

But the Loft split up for ideological reasons it seems, and Art left The Loft and began The Cellar. Perhaps because Art was a live and let live hip kind of guy. He wanted to do it! Whatever he thought would let it happen. Art would paint a painting in an hour if somebody was coming to buy it. It was an original, you dig?

He was open in that way to many kinds of liberalism, and most comfortable with his own. But The Cellar, when it was dealing was where it was. Like Art, himself, somewhat interior, for all that chatter, but the shadowy descent to where he dealt, was filled with beautiful feelings and ideas, transforming images.

I will always hold the Cellar close in memory. I went to see Sun Ra there and fell in love with Sylvia Robinson, now Amina Baraka, my wife.

Can you imagine Sun Ra in the shadowy hip substance of the

Harold "Mhisani" Wilson (1934-1980)

Statement at Harold Wilson Memorial
August 31, 1980

WHY DID MHISANI DIE?

He died. He was murdered, by our weakness. He was killed because we have not learnt yet how to destroy our enemies. And so they continue to destroy us.

WHO ARE OUR ENEMIES?

Our enemies, first of all, are this society, this system we live in, where we suffer from National Oppression and Racism, both of which are based on Monopoly Capitalism! This society where we were brought as slaves.

We have **never** had democracy in America! We have **never** been equal in America. Mhisani died because Niggers **sposed** to die in America. That's normal! America Murders Them!

America was built on Black murders, Black slavery. It got big on Black discrimination, Black segregation, Black unemployment, Black miseducation and no education, on systematic robbery and denial of rights, in short, on Black National Oppression, Racism, and super exploitation.

BUT BLACK YOUTH KILLED HIM (some people will say) ARE THEY OUR ENEMIES?

If we do not change this system, if we do not destroy it and rebuild another system where all people are really equal, then we will continue to be murdered by the sick one that exists! If we do not eliminate a system in which 40% of us can be unemployed, a system in which 50% of our children do not even finish high school, and rebuild a system in which all can be employed and all can be educated, then "our children" will continue to kill us.

We must build a system where all can live in Short Hills, if there's gonna be a Short Hills. Can't be some in the projects and some in Short Hills. If some gotta live in projects all need to live in projects. If anybody got money we all need to have money. Can't be some with money most with none. We got to build an equal society and until we build a truly equal society, we gonna be the ones who ain't equal.

There's no equality now. We at the bottom. Anybody says this society's free and equal is rich, sick or foolish! And when we **won't** fight our enemy we fight each other. When we don't struggle to **change** society, then society's evil changes us and makes us as evil as it is!

What do our youth have to look forward to? What have we provided for them? Can you get them a job? Can you get them an education? Can you get them a decent place to live? Can you provide them with a reason to be proud of you or themselves? What are the values they live by? They live by the values of capitalism and Black national oppression, they live by the values of racism. Which are oppression, self hatred, frustration, backwardness, greed, individualism. So called "Black on Black" Crime takes the place of struggle. Disco takes the place of accomplishment. "Freaky Deeky" takes the place of love. Drugs take the place of learning. The whole society has moved to the right, more backward more oppressive and we have moved to the right as well.

In 1970 we thought we had liberated ourselves, but liberation will only come from revolution! We didn't even get the best we could under capitalism, because we didn't understand class analysis, we didn't pick a Black revolutionary to lead us, we elected a Black stooge, a messenger boy, a peanut farmer! So we got drugged. We got alienated. We got apathetic. We got disillusioned. We said nothing is worth anything. Nothing more can be done. I'm thru struggling, Yiippee! & came running back to America.

Mhisani was our friend and is our guide, because he never stopped. We must take up his spirit and carry the struggle on to the end. Mhisani was building a Black United Front and we must continue his work. A United Front of all the different ideologies of Black people that exist in our community. Christian, Muslim, Nationalist, Communist, Democrat, Republican, we all have to unite around those things we have in common. Unite against bad housing. Unite against Crime. Unite Against Unemployment.

Unite against bad education. Unite against bad health care. Unite against police brutality. Unite against racism and National Oppression. Unite and fight back. Unite and struggle. Unite and make change. That's the only change coming, coming through struggle.

Our friend was killed because we stopped struggling. We must continue to build the Central Ward Community Center as a focus for our Unity, as a focus for struggle. As a catalyst for change. We must build a nonsectarian center, where all who are willing to unite, all who are willing to struggle can come together and carry on the struggle to the end.

There's work to do brothers and sisters, work to do, real work. The work of unifying and struggling is the real work. Can't make change otherwise. Can't uphold our dear friend's memory otherwise. Otherwise we can't make change, we can't transform this murdering system. The old society, the society that killed Mhisani must die and a new society must be born. All of you know that's what our friend, Mhisani, Harold, Hassan, wanted. And if you don't act on this knowledge, let it be known right now and out front that you will be slandering Harold Wilson's Memory!

LONG LIVE THE FIGHTING SPIRIT OF BROTHER HAROLD WILSON!
SELF DETERMINATION FOR THE AFRO-AMERICAN NATION!

1980

Larry Neal (1937-1981) and Bob Marley (1945-1981)

Wailers

(For Larry Neal and Bob Marley)

Wailers are we
We are Wailers. Don't get scared.
Nothing happening but out and way out.
Nothing happening but the positive. (Unless you the
negative.) Wailers. We wailers. Yeh, Wailers.
We wail, we wail.
    We could dig Melville on his ship
    confronting the huge white mad beast
    speeding death cross the sea to we.
    But we whalers. We can kill whales.
    We could get on top of a whale
    and wail. Wailers. Undersea defense hot folk
Blues babies humming when we arrive. Boogie ladies strumming our
black violet souls. Rag daddies come from the land of never say die.
Reggae workers bringing the funk to the people of I. We wailers all
    right.

Hail to you Bob, man! We will ask your question all our lives.
Could You Be Loved? I and I understand. We see the world
Eyes and eyes say Yes to transformation. Wailers. Aye, Wailers.
Subterranean night color Magis, working inside the soul of the world.
Wailers. Eyes seeing the world's being.

Hey, Bob, Wail on rock on Jah come into us as real vision and action
Hey, Larry, Wail on, with Lester and the Porkpie, wailing us energy
for truth. We Wailers is all, and on past that to say, wailing for all
we worth. Rhythm folks obsessed with stroking what is with our
sound purchase.

Call me Thelonius, in my crowded Wail Vessel, I hold the keys to
the funk kingdom. Lie on me if you want to, tell folks its yours
But for real wailing not tale telling, the sensitive know who the
Wailers be. Be We. Be We. We Wailers. Blue Blowers. The Real
Rhythm Kings.
We sing philosophy. Hambone precise findings. Image Masters of
the syncopated. Wailers & Drummers.
    Wailers & Trumpet stars.
    Wailers & Box cookers.
    Wailers & Sax flyers.
    Wailers & Bass thumpers.
    Wailers and Hey, wail, wail. We Wailers!
    Trombone benders. Magic singers.
    Ellingtonians.
The only Tranes faster than rocket ships. Shit.
Cut a rocket in our pocket and put a chord on the wall of the wind.
Wailers. Can you dig Wailing?

Call Me Bud Powell. You wanna imitate this?
Listen. Spree dee deet sprree deee whee spredeee whee deee

My calling card. The dialectic of silence.
The Sound approach.
Life one day will be filled even further with we numbers we song
But primitive place now, we wailing be kept underground.

But keep it in mind. Call me something Dukish. Something
Sassy.
Call me by my real name. When the world change
We wailing be in it, help make it, for real time.

Call Me. I call you. We call We.
Say, Hey Wailers. Hey, Wailers.
Hey hey hey, Wailers. Wail On!

Larry Neal (1937-1981)

The Wailer

I met Larry Neal in New York City as the Civil Rights Movement was turning into the Black Liberation Movement. That is, as the non-violent struggle for democracy led by Dr. King was being superceded by the sector of the movement inspired by Malcolm X, who called for Self-Determination, Self-Respect, and Self-Defense.

I first met Larry as a political comrade, as part of the swelling numbers of young people raised watching Dr. King beaten and assaulted, leading the masses in struggle against American *Apartheid*.

We came together, with a number of others, seeking to raise the level of black struggle to a more intense expression. We were young people who responded to the assassination of Patrice Lumumba by taking to the street, even invading the U.N. (way back when the U.S. controlled it) to show our opposition to U.S. imperialism.

[And it is important that we realize the pattern of their murders, in U.S. imperialism's attempt to stop the international rise of Black Liberation and Liberation Movements in general. When the hot spot of the Black Liberation Movement was Africa, Lumumba, Sylvanus Olympio, Mondlane, Cabral, were assassinated. When it moved to the U.S., Malcolm, King, Medgar Evers, Fred Hampton, and countless numbers of others. And now, the hot spot is the Caribbean, with the murders of Walter Rodney, Mikey Smith, Maurice Bishop, the mystery surrounding Bob Marley's death!]

We were young people on the move politically. No, we would not turn the other cheek. No, we would not be passive in our resistance. Malcolm was our man, our voice. Self-Defense! We would fight.

Men like Rob Williams were heroes to us. Resisting and disarming the Klan. Threatening **Them**!

We would show these "crackers" (a term I learned from my Republican grandfather) that the days of their torture of black people, anywhere!, were long gone. We would fight. We would arm ourselves and fight.

Larry was there. Young, hip, talking black revolution. Clean as, and like the rest of us, arrogant as, the afternoon sun. Hot and brightly shining. Full of life, energy, and Black Fire!

I found out Larry was an artist, a poet, writer, after our mutually expressed commitment to destroy white supremacy. It was the same with Askia Toure. We met fighting police while protesting Lumumba's murder. We found out we both wrote poetry, afterwards!

It was part of our commitment to the black revolutionary democratic struggle that we collaborated to create the Black Arts Repertory Theater School [BARTS] in Harlem. Both Larry and Askia were among the chief catalysts for that blazing and progressive, though short-lived, institution.

But the institution set a concrete example for the movement— it was part of *The Black Arts Movement!*—the movement by young, black artists in the '60s, to create an art, a literature, that would fight for black people's liberation with as much intensity as Malcolm X, our "Fire Prophet," and the rest of the enraged masses who took to the streets in Birmingham after the four little girls had been murdered by the Klan and FBI, or the ones who were dancing in the street in Harlem, Watts, Newark, Detroit.

We wanted an art that would actually reflect black life and its history and legacy of resistance and struggle! We wanted an art that was as black as our music. A blues poetry (a la Langston and Sterling); a jazz poetry; a funky verse full of exploding anti-racist weapons. A bebop and new music poetry, that would scream and taunt and rhythm—attack the enemy into submission. An art that would educate and unify black people in our attack on an anti-black racist America. We wanted a *mass art*, an art that could "Monkey" out the libraries and "Boogaloo" down the street in tune with popular revolution. A poetry the people could sing as they beat Faubus and Wallace and Bull Connor to death!

What we wanted to create would be African American and Revolutionary. In fact, it would be the real link in our history, part of the mainstream of black art through the century. Although we were not clear enough in our logical and spiritual antecedents; e.g., if we had only read Langston's *The Negro Artist and the Racial Mountain* in high school, many of the twists and turns of our quest for self-understanding would have been short cut. The movement at still higher levels.

Larry was an innovator in that regard. He was a spiritual leader of that movement. One of the hot lipped hip bebop poetry warriors trying to take the language someplace else, just as King and Malcolm were trying to take the whole society someplace else. Just as Jesse is trying to take the place into space today!

I felt almost immediately a close connection with Larry. We were very much alike in a lot of ways. Artists who wanted to make revolution. Revolutionary intellectuals. Trying to bring our bebop love into the streets of rebellion.

And throughout the existence of the BARTS Larry was a constant source of intelligence and inspiration. We demanded a lot from ourselves, but finally did not have the science at our disposal to transform rebellion into revolution. Yet the direction, the intention; e.g., the need for black institutions that would carry and reinterpret the revolutionary democratic black imperative in the U.S. Carry and sustain it, create it, generation after generation, at yet higher levels. The need for them still exists. Even worse now than in the '60s, when the spontaneous fire of the people overturned reaction and backwardness. Yet nothing can be accomplished just by spontaneous struggle. There must be scientific ideology and scientific organization. The BARTS is where we first learned that in quite painful fashion. In fact when I left Harlem, under duress of ignorance and the FBI, Larry was shot for attempting to maintain revolutionary integrity in the face of provocateurs and scum.

But what is so important is that because our words were words created by revolutionary passion, the inspiration, the focus, the skills we had as artists expanded by our very commitment to revolution. Larry Neal and Askia Toure were my models in the mid-'60s for Black Art. We wanted the oral tradition in our work, we wanted the sound, the pumping rhythm of black music. The signifying drawl of blues. Larry incorporated it all into his work. High intelligence, revolutionary commitment, and great skill. Which is why it infuriates me when I hear young economist artists (as Lenin termed them) more interested in careerism and getoverism than black liberation, try to put down the artists of the '60s for lack of skills. What dismally brainwashed opportunistic vulture feces.

As if it took no skill to move the people, to have the black masses wailing our love songs to self-determination, self-respect and self-defense, as they struggled to change the world. It took much more skill, it takes much more skill, to move the people, than it does simply to stand in the bossman's payline to get a gig as occasionally mentioned whore in the national lie. Which is where a lot of folks have gone, in collaborative celebration of the steady deadly move to fascism and nuclear war set forth as examples of human dignity by the fascist-minded Ronald Reagan and his white supremacy *über alles* regime!

Art does not have to be philosophically and ideologically reactionary. It is possible (and necessary) to struggle for human development, for liberation and social transformation in art. We do not have to create *Birth of a Nation* or the *Cantos* to be great artists. We do not have to support fascists or white supremacy to be "immortal." Only the bourgeoisie, the ignorant, or servants of the above, think this. Larry did not think it.

Ghost Poem #1

(Larry Neal, Winter, 1971, *Hoodoo Hollerin' Bebop Ghosts*)

You would never shoot smack
or lay in one of these Harlem
doorways pissing on yourself
that is not your way   not the
way of Alabama boys groomed slick
for these wicked cities momma
warned us of
You were always swifter than that:
the fast money was the Murphy game

or the main supply before the cutting,
so now you lean with the shadows
(at the dark end of Turk's bar)
aware that the hitman is on your ass

You know that there is something inevitable
about it
You know that he will come   as sure as shit
snorting blow for courage
and he will burn you at the peak of your peacocking
glory
And when momma gets the news
she will shudder over the evening meal
and moan: "Is that my Junie Boy runnin
with that fast crowd?"

During the BARTS period, Larry was also one of the featured
writers in *Liberator Magazine*, published by Dan Watts, which
was one of the most progressive periodicals of the period. Larry's
literary criticism, and his political commentary were incisive signal flags of our movement. Teaching us and goading us and giving
us hope and information. Larry was not only a poet and essayist,
he wrote drama and screenplays. One of our most important col-
laborations was the anthology *Black Fire* (now out of print)
which collected the key black artists of the period, young and fire
hot, to show the way the Black Arts movement spelled out. But,
obviously, in this present period, such an anthology is economi-
cally banned as too far out, too hot, too "racist," man them niggers were crazy, et cetera. But the book set the tone and direction
for the literary revolution in progress. And Larry's hand was key
in the shaping of that work.

We also collaborated later on the magazine *Cricket*, a publication devoted to African American music (wish we had it today).
Larry was one of the editors, along with A. B. Spellman and
myself. It had only three issues, but they were significant in that,
for the first time, black people were defining their art, their aesthetic, their social and aesthetic ideology, not someone else's. Both

these publications were black nationalist. As were Larry and myself and countless others, during the period. Many of us have moved to the left since that period. And some of our metaphysics and crass cultural nationalism is embarrassing even to us, but the essence of the work, was resistance to imperialism, resistance to white supremacy, even in its flawed form. Our Hearts were Good! Good & Black!

Such institutions as the BARTS and *Cricket*, even the publishing of African American artists, is still critical for us, especially in a backward period such as this. But our lack of institutions, itself, contributes to the backwardness!

You see our traditions, which we are often late to understand, if we persevere as intellectuals or continue them naturally and spontaneously as part of the mass culture and intelligence, our traditions, the politics, art, culture of the African American people, have always been, in the main, *democratic* and because of this, in the context of chattel slavery, reaction, white supremacy, racism, national oppression, our traditions are *revolutionary*.

(We have yet to experience bourgeois democracy. It still amazes me to hear Americans talk about this place, because, to paraphrase Langston, "America never was America / to me.")

That revolutionary democratic (yet highly elegant) tradition was what Larry Neal carried and upheld. Shit, to look at Larry, with his ultra-hip Philadelphia self, was to look at the *art* of being oneself. His very sartorial splendor was a *statement*, both obvious and profound. One that alto artist Arthur Blythe confirms as *In The Tradition*!

Too many black intellectuals forfeit this tradition brainwashed and humiliated by their negro *training*, which they mistake as education. We get degrees in other, from other, to be always very other than ourselves or somebody our grandmama would *recognize* as righteous carriers of the spirit which animated those "Black and Unknown Bards."

Larry came at a period of rising political intensity, struggle and consciousness. He passed it on, like the black baton of our history, to any who knew him or was moved or influenced by him, by anyone who could read.

Because Larry Neal, when all the shouting and lying is done, perhaps when there really is a *free world* (contrary to white racist bully imperialism's definition of that non-existent paradigm), Larry will emerge as one of the truly *wonderful* artists of our age. A great poet, visionary essayist, and important dramatist. Even as he is known *now* by those of us sufficiently disconnected from the aesthetic of dying murderers to appreciate truth made beautiful!

Poppa Stoppa Speaks from His Grave
(Larry Neal, 1969, *Hoodoo Hollerin' Bebop Ghosts*)

Remember me baby in my best light,
lovely hip style and all;
all laid out in my green velour
stashing on corners
in my boxcar coat,
so sure of myself, too cool for words,
and running down a beautiful game.

It would be super righteous
if you would think of me that way sometimes;
and since it can't be that way,
just the thought of you digging on me that way
would be hip and lovely even from here.
Yeah, you got a sweet body, baby,
but out this way, I won't be needing it;
but remember me and think of me
that way sometimes.

But don't make it no big thing though;
don't jump jive and blow your real romance.
but in a word, while you high-steppin and finger-poppin
tell your lovin' man that I was a bad
motherfucker till the Butcher cut me down.

Now, three years after Larry's tragic premature death, this conference is important and it is made even more so by its carrying his name. And by so doing, hopefully, helping to spread and revive the power and relevance of Larry's art and political message.

Today, we are in a reactionary period, similar to the 1880s when, after the Civil War and the abortive attempt at Reconstruction, black people were betrayed by almost every segment of the American population and thrown down into the neo-slavery of sharecropping and separate but evil American Apartheid.

The period Larry Neal and I came to consciousness in was a highly political, highly progressive period. Twenty years later, after the multiple assassinations of our leaders, the cointelpro wrecking of our movement, we see the very people that murdered Malcolm, Martin (and for that matter John and Robert Kennedy) sitting in the White House trying to murder the world!!

We see people who used to call themselves revolutionaries trying to cleave their way into the Mormon church, or writing barbecue cookbooks, or hidden away somewhere trying to be cool in the face of monsters. This is not in the spirit of Larry Neal, nor is it in the great tradition of the African American people.

It is significant this conference, the second, should come now when there is some sign of a reawakening and reconstruction of the movement. Jesse Jackson's candidacy is straight ahead in the tradition of resistance and struggle that has characterized the African American spirit. People want to know why Jesse Jackson speaks in rhymes. Black leaders have to be poets, otherwise the people wouldn't listen! Because the mainstream of black poetry has always touched and been touched by that revolutionary democratic spirit and was therefore always close to the people and close to the movement. This is what Larry Neal's art was all about. It was like the mass line that Mao Zedong talks about, "From the people to the people." We use our skill and the people's fire.

We opposed the dead literature of the dying criminal imperialist culture because that literature is a method of recruiting us into the empire of exploitation and oppression or madness and irrelevance.

Sound, Light, Heat, Spirit, Rhythm, Movement, Transformation, not criminal boredom and irrelevance, not support of what cannot be supported.

Larry's work is universal because the human spirit struggling for revelation/revolution is seen across the world. The greatest artists of any culture are those upholding the upward motion of the human spirit, the will of the majority to transform the world and itself in that world.

The spirit Larry Neal's work will contain forever is the spirit of the world constantly being reborn, of renaissance and new life. It is a spirit that will motivate the billions of us until the planet explodes.

The many tasks and treks and acts Larry speaks of, will speak of, still need to be accomplished. The raising of consciousness, the opposition to reaction, the needs for institutions and a revolutionary art are still priorities needed to be brought into reality.

If we do not build revolutionary institutions, for instance, Larry Neal's works might disappear or become obscure. They will not be honored by our enemies, just as freedom ain't never been free.

Larry is an example for us. Read his work. Heed his example and imperatives. Understand why he was so hip. It is all critical and necessary. As we pass the baton from generation to generation. We see our cultural workers falling on all sides. Suicided by imperialism. Larry Neal, dead of a heart attack, age 43.

It means we have not created what we need to preserve ourselves and kill our enemies. It means we are still in the middle passage. Let us honor our fallen comrade and brother Larry Neal, by honoring his work and bringing into reality its demanding vision!!!

Don't Say Goodbye To The Porkpie Hat

for Mingus, Bird, Prez, Langston, and them

Don't say goodbye to the Porkpie Hat that rolled
along on nodded shoulders
that swang bebop phrases
in Minton's jelly roll dreams
Don't say goodbye to hip hats tilted in the style of a

soulful era;
   the Porkpie Hat that Lester dug
   swirling in the sound of sax blown suns
               phrase on phrase, repeating bluely
               tripping in and under crashing
               hi-hat cymbals, a fickle girl
               getting sassy on the rhythms.

   Musicians heavy with memories
   move in and out of this gloom;
   the Porkpie Hat reigns supreme
   smell of collard greens
   and cotton madness
   commingled in the nigger elegance of the style.

   The Porkpie Hat sees tonal memories

   of salt peanuts and hot house birds

   the Porkpie Hat sees . . .
   Cross riffing square kingdoms, riding midnight Scottsboro
   trains. We are haunted by the lynched limbs.
   On the road:
   It would be some hoodoo town
   It would be some cracker place
   you might meet redneck lynchers
   face to face
   but mostly you meet mean horn blowers
   running obscene riffs
   Jelly Roll spoke of such places:
   the man with the mojo hand
   the dyke with the .38
   the yaller girls
   and the knifings.

   Stop-time Buddy and Creole Sydney
   wailed in here. Stop time. *   *

chorus repeats, stop and shuffle.
stop and stomp.
listen to the horns, ain't they mean?
now ain't they mean
in blue
in blue
in blue streaks of mellow wisdom
blue notes
coiling around
the Porkpie Hat
and ghosts of dead musicians drifting through
here on riffs that smack
of one-leg trumpet players
and daddy glory piano ticklers
who
twisted arpeggios
with diamond-flashed fingers.
There was Jelly Roll Morton, the sweet mackdaddy,
hollering Waller, and Willie The Lion Smith,
some mean showstoppers.

Ghosts of dead holy rollers ricocheted in the air funky
with white lightnin' and sweat.
Emerald bitches shot shit in a kitchen smelling
of funerals and fried chicken.
Each city had a different sound:
there was Mambo, Rheba, Jeanne;
holy the voice of these righteous sisters.
Shape to shape, horn to horn
the Porkpie Hat resurrected himself
night to night, from note to note
skimming the horizons, flashing bluegreenyellow lights
and blowing black stars
and weird looneymoon changes, chords coiled about him
and he was flying
fast
zipping

past
sound
into cosmic silences.
And yes
and caresses flowed from the voice in the horn in the blue
of the yellow whiskey room where bad hustlers with big
coats moved, digging the fly sister, fingerpopping while
tearing at chicken and waffles.

The Porkpie Hat loomed specter-like, a vision for the world:
shiny, the knob toe shoes,
sporting hip camel coats
and righteous pin stripes,
pants pressed razor shape;
and caressing his horn, baby like.

So we pick up our axes and prepare
to blast the white dream;
we pick up our axes
re-create ourselves and the universe,
sounds splintering the deepest regions
of spiritual space
crisp and moaning voices
leaping in the horns of destruction,
blowing death and doom to all who have no use for the spirit.

So we cook out of sight
into cascading motions of joy delight
shooflies the Bird lolligagging
and laughing for days,
and the rhythms way up in there
wailing, sending scarlet rays, luminescent,
spattering bone and lie.
we go on cool lords
wailing on into star nights,
rocking whole worlds, unfurling song on song
into long stretches of green spectral shimmerings,

blasting on, fucking the moon with the blunt edge
of a lover's tune, out there now, joy riffing
for days and do
railriding and do
talking some lovely shit and do
to the Blues God who blesses us.

No, don't say goodbye to the Porkpie Hat,
he lives, oh yes.
Lester lives and leaps
Delancey's dilemma is over
Bird lives
Lady lives
Eric stands next to me
while I finger the Afro-horn
Bird lives
Lady lives
Lester leaps in every night
Tad's delight
is mine now
Dinah knows
Richie knows
that Bud is Buddha
that Jelly Roll dug juju
and Lester lives
in Ornette's leapings
the Blues God lives
we live
live
spirit lives
and sound lives
bluebird lives
lives and leaps
dig the mellow voices
dig the Porkpie Hat
dig the spirit in Sun Ra's sound
dig the cosmic Trane

dig be
dig be
dig be
spirit lives in sound
dig be
sound lives in spirit
dig be
yeah!!!
spirit lives
spirit lives
spirit lives
SPIRIT!!!
SWHEEEEEEEEEEEEEEETTT!!!

take it again
this time from the top

Okot p'Bitek (1931-1982)

Brother Okot

Our people say
death lives
in the West
(Any one
can see
    plainly, each evening
where the sun
goes to die)

      So Okot
      is now in the West

      Here w/ us
      in hell

    I have heard
    his songs
    felt the earth
    drum his
    dance
his wide ness
& Sky self

    Ocoli Singer
    Ocoli Fighter

        * * *

Brother Okot
now here w/us
in the place

Where even the Sun
  dies.

                                              1983

Owen Dodson (1914-1983)

Owen Dodson

Owen was a singular man as poet, dramatist, cultural historian and teacher. He was a man who could be as drenched in hauteur and aloof elegance as he could be warm and expansive.

For years Owen was the heart and soul of Howard University's fabled Howard Players, and even those of us who did not perform with the Players were made deeply proud by their internationally recognized exploits and associated ourselves with them and regarded Owen as their leader, as indeed he was.

One incident that Owen was fond of relating happened at Howard in the mid-'60s, just after I had received some recognition or was it notoriety for the play, *Dutchman*. I was invited back to Howard for a performance of the play there. But during the performance, I realized that someone had bowdlerized the work and removed all the, then, dirty words, which of course nowadays one may hear even on television.

After the performance, I was asked to speak, and as I made my address I recited a litany of the banished cuss words to the burning chagrin of some of the old guard Howard petty bourgeoisie. But seated to one side of the stage and literally rolling in the aisles was Owen, apparently happy that someone had managed to make some of those stiff Negroes turn something like red. Owen never ceased to retell that story.

Owen's loss makes us all losers—it is very hard to express the depth of the vacuum left by the disappearance of one of our major cultural workers. He was an aspect of Black art and culture we tended to take for granted. And the loss we feel now is only a beginning;, it will get even deeper. Though we should be moved and ecstatic that we ever got to know the man and his work at all!!

1983

Michael Smith (1954-1983)

Bloody Neo-Colonialism
or
The Murder of Mikey Smith
or
The Murder of Walter Rodney
or
The Murder of Maurice Bishop

(delivered at Michael Smith Memorial, November 3, 1983,
Brixton, London)

I want you to think about a world where it is impossible for Black people, anywhere, to develop an intelligentsia, in the fullest and profoundest sense of that term, without them being assaulted, and in too many cases, murdered! Why? Because to be a Black intellectual, since the slave trade began, is to be a consciousness that not only understands the historic oppression of the Black people worldwide, but also has some clarity about what must be done to end that oppression!

The poet, Michael Smith, was such a consciousness, and not idly, his poetry speaks directly to those two levels of our most developed minds—understanding the oppression and understanding what must be done about it. The most developed of such intellectuals also understands that such realization is sterile unless it is a blueprint for action!

Why was Michael Smith destroyed? Only because of our collective weakness. That we have developed this intelligentsia, not only in the Caribbean, but all over the Black world, but have not organized sufficiently to protect them! !

In the last generation, we could mention Lumumba, Cabral, Nkrumah, Sibeko in Africa. We could mention Malcolm X, Martin Luther King, Medgar Evers, Fred Hampton in the U.S.

And now, very recently, in a brutal sickening rapid succession,

Walter Rodney, Mikey Smith, Maurice Bishop in the Caribbean!

Revolutionary Black intellectuals are dangerous to the status quo of superpower imperialist domination throughout the world, because all over the world, Black people are at the bottom of these racist imperialist societies. Not only is imperialism a worldwide system, but since the primitive accumulation of capital needed to develop modern capitalism, including the industrial revolution, was based on the African slave trade, the social **order** of imperialist societies is not only based on national oppression and class exploitation, but **caste** as well. So that the darker one is, the more completely one is victimized by monopoly capitalism and imperialism. The sharper we are attacked by racism.

Particularly in the third world, Africa, Asia, the Middle East, Latin America, since the revolutionary intellectuals, historically, **traditionally**, have tried to guide their people toward social transformation, material liberation, self-determination, scientific socialism, they have always come under sharp attack by the rulers.

For Black people, such attacks will always be more brutal and murderous because of our position at the bottom of these societies. But now imperialism has evolved to the stage of **neocolonialism**, where no longer are we ruled directly by the hand of European colonialism, but now, in most cases, we are ruled by imperialism indirectly, through what Amilcar Cabral called "native agents."

Throughout the third world, imperialism rules now mostly through native agents. So that Neruda is murdered by Pinochet; Ngugi is imprisoned by Kenyatta, driven into exile by Arap Moi. Mikey Smith is murdered by CIAga, Walter Rodney destroyed by Forbes Burnham.*

In the U.S., where the African American people have never been in a colonial situation but have existed since the 19th century as an **oppressed nation** within a nation, today in many of the

---

*Forbes Burnham was Prime Minister of Guyana when Walter Rodney (a Caribbean dissident) was killed in an explosion in his car. Government officials alleged—falsely—that Rodney had been trying to purchase a bomb and it exploded.

26 large cities we live in, there are Black mayors who too often serve as messengers from Ronald Reagan and little else.

But in the Caribbean, particularly, we have seen for the last few years how thoroughly ruled by neo-colonialism that region is! Since the age of colonialism, (i.e., open direct foreign domination) has mostly been past, in the Caribbean U.S. imperialism sees that its interests are served by spineless running dogs who resemble the oppressed people we selves!

And while we rejoiced at the passing of colonialism, though we must still kill it dead in the Black world, in South Africa, Namibia and in the Caribbean, in Puerto Rico, its successor and higher stage, neo-colonialism, has proven to be even more dangerous, since all too often it dupes the oppressed people that they are free and independent! While those of us who try to take the lead toward real independence and self-determination are brutally attacked by imperialism in a variety of ways and often totally eliminated!

Black oppression and submission are still key elements in the existing world order. Africa is a neo-colonial travesty, subordinated north and south by racist settler colonies, Israel and South Africa! The few progressive states are constantly in danger.

The third world is too poor to afford bourgeois democracy in the U.S. and European model, though they must give lip-service to it. So that most times there is not even the facade or illusion of representative democracy, the way people are tricked it exists in the "metropoles." In the third world, resistance to the neo-colonial order is met with swift violent death. The niceties and trappings of bourgeois democracy, trial by jury, appeals, freedom of speech, etc. are not even pretended toward.

So that in Guyana, Walter Rodney's militant leadership of the *Working People's Association* is stopped suddenly and permanently by the bloody neo-colonial fiend, Forbes Burnham. Rodney's crime: working to build an authentic scientific socialism, as opposed to the gibberish and nonsense spouted by Burnham to cover his exploitation of the Guyanese people.

The tragedy of this assassination has still not totally been absorbed by us. Rodney was one of our most brilliant leaders.

How long before he is replaced? What vacuum and suffering exist because of this? Why were we not better **organized** to prevent this?

In Jamaica, Michael Manley's confused social democracy is overthrown by U.S. imperialism. That is another loss in the sense that even those slim gains, represented by the Manley government, must now be recovered. Manley's replacement, Seaga, is an open agent of U.S. imperialism and part of the new even more reactionary order set in motion by the rise to power of the right wing regime of Ronald Reagan in the U.S.

It is under such a regime, in such a reactionary period, when Mikey Smith can be murdered. Reagan openly sanctions such attacks. His whole regime is based on the philosophy that the rising tide of revolution, seen throughout the world since WW2, must be stopped!

What must be done to a Black revolutionary consciousness in openly neo-colonial Jamaica, when the television ads say to millions of Americans, "**Come Back to Jamaica**; things are like they used to be, the niggers have been put back in their places, come to Jamaica. Sun and Fun, while the native niggers are made to eat even more shit than before!"

What must be done to a revolutionary consciousness that speaks directly of the people's suffering and the causes of that suffering? A revolutionary consciousness that even dares to openly criticize the rulers in front of the people and walk the streets, nightly singing that criticism to whoever will listen!?

This is why the revolutionary consciousness in artists is especially dangerous, because they can put revolution into the hearts and minds of the people with a simple melody! (I am still not satisfied with official stories of how Bob Marley died—cancer of the toe?)

And did you notice the hypocrite Seaga babble about pardoning Marcus Garvey as a dumb gesture of guilt in connection with Mikey Smith's assassination by his Heathens!?

Mikey Smith's poetry was important not only because it addressed itself, with its content, to the needs of the people, and opposed the people's enemies; its form also was a revolutionary innovation in the way it sought to use the speech of the people.

The poetry did not seek to imitate the rulers, as those Negroes do who get the rulers' prizes. Mikey Smith's poetry spoke the truth in the rhythms and accents of the masses. This is why his poetry was so dangerous to imperialism. This is why the whole dub poetry movement is so important. This is why Reggae is so important. The artist can make truth irresistible!

But still we must ask, in these brutal dangerous times, how much longer will we go on largely unorganized and vulnerable to our enemies? Ronald Reagan, everyday, moves the whole world closer to fascism and WW3, how are we organized to stop it?

The murder of Maurice Bishop and his cabinet stinks of the U.S. CIA! Another brilliant young Black revolutionary intellectual slaughtered by imperialism.

And no matter what internal struggles we may hear happened in Grenada, nothing can justify the U.S. invasion! But it is one more long stride by Reagan and U.S. imperialism toward fascism domestically and nuclear war internationally!

Reagan, and the extreme right wing ideologues of the sector of the U.S. bourgeoisie he represents, seem determined to regain world domination, in constant contention with the other super-power, the USSR, or blow up the world trying!

U.S. intervention in El Salvador; attempts to destabilize and eventually overthrow the democratic Nicaraguan government; the occupation of Lebanon in support of an unrepresentative fascist government and now the invasion of Grenada—these events should make it clear that the first shots of WW3 are already being fired!!!

Reagan lies when he says U.S. marines invaded Grenada to save U.S. citizens. Those students were in no danger. It is an utterly transparent lie!

And to say that the U.S. has invaded to restore democratic, institutions, while at the same time violating the U.S. Constitution by banning U.S. press coverage of the invasion, should speak directly to how far to the right U.S. society is moving and how domestic fascism must accompany international imperialist war.

What Reagan wants is to make Grenada like the Black ghettoes of the U.S. with their 40% unemployment rate, and ubiquitous dope addicts. Are these democratic institutions? Since Reagan has not invaded South Africa to restore democratic institutions in that racist settler colony, we can presume that he includes South Africa in his definition of "the Free World."

The invasion of Grenada was not only an example of naked imperialist aggression, it also reeks of racism and white supremacy. Since, in all other cases in the last years, U.S. imperialism has used stooges and surrogates to undermine, destabilize or overthrow progressive regimes in the third world. But in the case of small Black Grenada, the effrontery of self-determination was too much for the racists in the White House to stand. Bishop had to be killed! The marines had to invade, and now we find out that an appointee of Queen Elizabeth II, Sir Paul Scoon, the so called Governor General, is nominally (i.e., the **house** slave) in charge. (Sir Paul Scoon?, well we've met his coon, now where is Sir Paul?)

And then, as we look on in horror, that horror changes to utter shame when we witness the crew of house niggers (**Charles**, Dominica; **Adams**, Barbados; **Seaga**, Jamaica; **Cato**, St. Vincent; **Compton**, St. Lucia; **Byrd**, Antigua) who jump up and down and applaud on cue, hoping to legitimize the invasion to Black eyes. As imperialism grows more desperate and wild, so its apologists must also get wilder and more bizarre in defending it!

Yes, the tide of revolution has been blunted many places in the world by the counter attack of U.S. imperialism, and with this same motion, as one aspect of U.S.-USSR international superpower contention, the danger of WW3 is even more possible.

But how shall we survive and how shall we eventually prevail? Certainly we must understand that the only weapon we have is **organization**! It is not enough to have a revolutionary consciousness, a revolutionary idea, we must build truly revolutionary organizations wherever we are to overthrow and eliminate the rule of monopoly capitalism, thereby smashing the material base of racism and national and sexual oppression. We must build organizations rooted in the masses, with close ties with those masses. Revolutionary organizations that link theory with practice. Organizations which are capable of criticism and self-criticism. Organizations which can build, as well as be a part of united fronts, wherein a majority of the people are focused on the destruction of our enemies. Organizations that can fight and help make revolution!

In the U.S., we need a multinational communist party which can lead the various popular movements and tie them together, in order to struggle more intensely against our common enemy, white racist monopoly capitalism! We must also begin work in the very near future to maximize Black voting strength, and as part of some national progressive coalition of all nationalities, get rid of Reagan in the next national elections!

But wherever we are, our movements can only be strengthened by strengthening our organizational capacity to resist and defeat imperialism. Black artists and intellectuals must organize themselves on a much higher level, according to the specific social context they exist in.

We must have organizations of revolutionary writers and painters as well as historians. We must build international support groups to assist in the crushing of South African colonialism, so that when the time comes we can turn whatever country we're in upside down, to make it impossible for the western governments to help the South African racists stop the Black revolution.

We must be able to counter attack against imperialism internationally and make hoodlums like Seaga and Baby Doc, or the neo-colonial surrogates that assisted Reagan's invasion, tremble and denounce their collaboration with imperialism. But we cannot do this without organization!

The murders of Rodney, Smith and Bishop speak directly to our lack of strong national and international organization among Black revolutionaries. The entire Black world should have been mobilized to speak out and condemn the monster, Burnham, for his assassination of Walter Rodney. The entire Black world, and through its influence, the entire civilized world, must be mobilized to condemn Seaga for his duplicity in the slaying of Mikey Smith.

But this requires progressive organization and the abandonment of petty bourgeois individualism, addiction to atavism and metaphysics among the artists and intellectuals, and a renewed commitment to struggle at the most scientific levels. And ultimately, we must be always working to build the true organizational instruments of scientific socialism, because unless monopoly capitalism is destroyed, conditions cannot exist in which racism and national oppression can be destroyed!

Unless we are willing to organize ourselves as revolutionary fighters, in command of the historic legacy of working class political analysis and led by the masses of people themselves, carrying our various national liberation and independence struggles through to the end, that is, all the way to *socialism*, we will always be tortured and weakened by the murders of our most brilliant brothers and sisters by our enemies.

Let us, in the name of Walter Rodney, organize in all the places we live, not only towards the liberation of ourselves, but as part of the whole population, where we live in multinational contexts, organize for the transformation of the whole society.

And let us, in the name of Maurice Bishop, fight imperialism and neo-colonialism and finally make revolution, so the majority can take power.

And finally let us, those of us who are intellectuals and artists, let us, in the name of Mikey Smith, develop as truly revolutionary intellectuals and revolutionary artists, whose works issue from the collective mind, memory and feelings of the people! Whose creations move through the world with the power of unstoppable truth, so that they will be celebrated even in the future, when finally there really is a Free World!

DEATH TO IMPERIALISM AND NEO-COLONIALISM!
LONG LIVE MIKEY SMITH!

Kimako Baraka (1936-1984)

Lanie Poo: Her Life, Her Death, Our World!!!

The failure of all of us in here is staggering! My self, particularly, to
have let my own sister, my only blood sister, expire, in brutish violence. At the morgue, my father stumbled backward, a cry broke
from his lips. That his only daughter, Sandra Elaine, i.e., Kimako,
i.e., "something wonderful," could be smashed broken destroyed.

> *And half our hearts*
> *& lives!*
> *But how did we get here?*
> *This tragedy clutching my*
> *speech*
>
> *& memory*
>
> *Our legacy as a people*
> *We Africans in America*

Because Kimako's destruction can only show how weak and
defenseless we are, how trusted in sickness.

The prisoners cry: "Let them stop it. Those others. They know.
Let them stop this. We can't move. We're frozen by the image of
our captivity. Let those others stop them, we can do nothing,"
except kill each other and ourselves!

Kimako made the ultimate mistake of wanting to be a creative
force in this rotten society. Of being moved by truth and beauty.
Of wanting to do nothing so much as Dance, to express the
rhythm of life as a part of that rhythm. And when she could no
longer do that, still she would be an actress. To "speak the
speech" that would uncover that which remains covered. To
enlighten and later to endarken. To express the deepness of
humanity, which can only be approached through ART

48

She thought, once she had made the decision to do these things, that nothing **wanted** to stop her. She thought she did not have to be a school teacher. As powerful a calling as that is, she did not want be do something after awhile merely to fill the list of middle-class norms that pass as life for many of the objectively nonliving.

Once she had gone past the curtain of self-doubt and limitation the undead want to drape us in, to insure we can never express what really matters in life, itself, its confirmation, what is real, what is alive, what is beautiful.

She did not understand, as I did not, when we were younger, that one aspect of Black national oppression is to be put in a jail of frustration, because whatever one wants to realize in life, if it is an expression of humanity, like a self-fulfilling vocation, you are supposed to forget that. That Black means slavery here. Be a slave or be . . . no you cannot be. It will not be allowed.

And then to be Black and female. Kimako wanted to be a director. She wanted to be on the stage. To dance to act. And when she cd no longer do these things, she wanted still to be close to them, to have a hand at bringing new meaning in the world, but you cannot be Black you cannot be female and aspire to creativity.

When she reached a higher level of national consciousness, as a result of the surge of the '60s, she could see clearly, by means of our truest guides Malcolm X, Martin Luther King, what she, what we all, are up against. So she put her hand to that struggle as well. She understood that the most important function of art is to tell the truth with such blinding force, such altering beauty, that the world itself is altered. That the noblest function of art is to force beauty into the world. To oppose ignorance and oppression. A word, a movement, a phrase of notes, arm, hand, fingers extended perhaps pointing the way. Stevie Wonder, of recent, is an example of the tradition of the Afro-American artist. The old "happy birthday" is dead. Stevie moved us by the millions to demand Dr. King's day.

Yet the slave demons of capitalism, racism, women's oppression demanded that for daring to say Blacks must be free, that Woman must be free, her life was forfeit. There was no way the powers that be were going to let her Direct. They would kill her first. No Black woman would be allowed to be a Black woman, a director, enthralled with truth and beauty. It could not be allowed. They would not permit it. They have put wormwood in some of our brains so that before we would dare attempt to be something forceful and positive, an expression of our historic tradition of resistance and struggle, we would sink deeper into the shadow void of "If Only."

Kimako tried to get jobs directing. She became one of the finest production stage managers in New York. She was Black and a woman. But whiteness and maleness is what is the aristocracy of the status quo. Not Blackness. Not femaleness. She must be forced back.

Too many already mind-destroyed-sycophants, even in colored skin, shout at us to stop trying to be free. To stop trying to create meaning to understand meaning in this world. Since the rulers demand our captivity our enthrallment with the status quo. Our worship of racism and male chauvinism, there are oppressed Negroes who also demand subservience from us. Who demand that our total lives' function be the worship of our oppression. Prisoners in love with their jailers, worshipers of Jail. Jailed minds. Jailed feelings.

For my part, what is so horrible is that, given the fact that I had a sister, only one sister of the blood, that the many plays I have written **should have** given her vehicles for her particular expression of our total collective lives. Kimako did act and direct some of these plays. But I should have created works for her. For Black women. To say and be, and all of us, therefore, would be. Our collective expression, raised again. In that African American tradition. In that democratic tradition reflected against a rainbow of nationalities and languages, telling of that growth through struggle of something beautiful, something wonderful (which was her name) which we know to be the positive legacy of our lives on the planet earth.

But Fanon says that some of the oppressed are made sick by oppression, and instead of killing our enemies, too often we want to be them. Being close to them makes the pathological feel more human, less oppressed, that they are allowed to be surrogates of the Not. No Yes, only No. Except Yes to slavery, sickness, Tommery.

Kimako's crime, for which the mad the sick the rulers had her destroyed, was wanting to be **genuinely human**, in spite of the madness that passes as sanity and respectability. Why don't you get a real job? A Director? Why don't you get a real job? Or worse, I've created these parts but they're not for you. You Black woman, you cannot be seen, you cannot take your rightful place, the rulers will not allow it, nor those sick quirks transformed from humanity into devilish tools of our supposed non-being. But we are being. Any way.

My sister was murdered to set an example of non-being for us, to intimidate us. To say to us, get a real job. As slave, stop trying to be. All she wanted, was to be in the theater. Was that so terrible that you cdn't permit it, you aweful money gods? Was that so terrible? You blinded white worshipping sycophants? You sick gobblers of death potions. You dead tiptoers around truth, you creators of lies, you mother liars and father you brother liars you Negro liars you white racist monopoly capitalist liars. You sick creeps crawling down the streets in the service of devil, murderers hired by pathology to rid the world of truth and beauty, who can only strike this one tiny woman down to try to frighten us. "Why should we feel sorry for you," the nigger reporter whines, "what with your politics?"

My sister was tiny, fragile, small, quiet, she laughed though, we had our codes that came up with us from youth, we cd talk to each other in ways we used when we were in the Secret Seven, with "Board," and Algie and Norman and Eddie and Dannie and Leroy and Laine. Under the porch plotting the overthrow of ugliness.

Get a real job. Get a wig. Be white, was the answer. All she wanted, my sister, Kimako, was to be in the theater. That's why she lived in the Manhattan Plaza, *New York Post*, she was a director, no matter your filth. She was an actress, a dancer, she had performed in hundreds of plays. Yet they distort this, because we cannot be allowed to be.

That's why, finally, unable to support herself the way she wanted as a beauty carrier a truth carrier, she stumbled into *AmWay*, short for the American Way. And found what is the American Way for the Black for the female, non-being. *AmWay* is like an American Pyramid Club with slightly cultish overtones. But you had to recruit people to form economic units for financial gain. This was a so-called real job. No, you can't be a director. That's why the *Post* had to question why my sister was even allowed in the Manhattan Plaza. The real job of Black women, according to these blood suckers, is prostitute, that's why the newspapers' implications. Outside of New York, it is even said by the wire services that I was a suspect in the murder!

A "Swank Pad" sd the *Post*, a government subsidized apt bldg for artists becomes a "swank pad" to complete the stereotype, to separate those of us who dare, from the rest. A swank pad. If Black people have two chairs and a table, how did they get it. It's a swank pad. You can't have good taste. You're a Black woman. It's a swank pad and you pick up drifters in bars or diners. Get a real job. Your real job is slave. Slaves. Slave. Get back. And the crazy brother, this hater, he's so crazy he showed up at the precinct "in a top hat" the *Post* says. Get a real job. Your job, Black activist, being mad.

My sister was brutally murdered, beaten to death, stabbed to death by an insane reflection of the real American dream, which is a nightmare. She was killed because instead of directing she was recruiting for *AmWay*. Now we cannot even open the coffin because we will not be intimidated even by the wanton destruction of this life so close to our hearts. We see here the way she looked. Sandi. Laine. Laney. Lanie Poo. Kimako. When she was director, producer, dancer, actress, Black activist. When she was director of the *House of Kuumba* (creativity). When she was proprietor and mover of Kimako's, with that wild image of the ancient Egyptian destroying Ronald Reagan, or was it Nixon or was it Attila the Hun, with a sharp unturnable sword. We see that smile. We feel that longing for truth. We feel that laughter in her brimming out, that warmth, that expressed humanity.

I began by citing our failure. What was it. That we have not created a context in which life can live, in which creativity can be spared and developed. That we have not built a world in which something wonderful and blessed, Kimako Baraka, could exist. Where life wd be sacred and protected. We cannot maintain something blessed and wonderful in this hell. We can, but we have not, and so we forfeit. Dr. King and Malcolm X were taken because we failed to protect them. My gentle fragile sister is dead because we failed to protect her. Because too many of us would rather worship our enemies, to raise them on high, to cover our sisters with images of devils.

It is clear that Lanie Poo could not make it, that Kimako could not live because we have created nothing which loves them and secures their lives, here in a world of pain. Lanie Poo needed a gun. Kimako needed an army of cultural workers. One strong brother would have helped. One blood relative not hypnotized by cave droppings, but alas, there was no one there the night Ronald Reagan sent his messenger of murder. None of us who claim to be strong or in love with truth and beauty. We were not there, too many times, repeated, we have not been where we were needed. Can it be true that we will have to live out the rest of our lives without something wonderful and blessed at our sides? We provided no food no sword no shield, just idle-words and turned backs, just the promise, that someday something else will be done. Can the rest of us swear that? That we will not be intimidated, that we will not continue to worship our enemies while mortgaging and collaborating in the murder of the blessed, the wonderful. I'll never say good bye to Kimako, I remember Lanie Poo, I remember my youth, I remember the promise, I've tried to make the commitment to transform this world. All of us who can say these things, let us fight, not submit, not stand on the side and demand purity in the face of ugly and do nothing about it but kill each other like dumb crabs in darkness afraid of the sun, silent in the face of insult and murder. No. **Remember Kimako.** Let me tell you about my gentle quiet sister, the dancer, the actress, the Black woman, her name was Kimako, something blessed and wonderful, before that she was called Lanie Poo.

Hey little girl, take care of yrself
she used to slip some vitamins in my hand
    when we parted
    take care of yrself
    get some rest, she'd say
    take care of yrself

Jesus Christ
    Not my sister . . . . . Oh No!!!

1984

Yusef Iman (1933-1984)

Our Man Yusef

Yusef came to The Black Arts shortly after we opened in Harlem, 1965. He had been with Malcolm before, even on that Sunday, February 21, when he was murdered!

Malcolm's murder unleashed a wave of Black response, adding to the deepening resistance raised from most Black people.

Yusef worked in and became one of the best known actors in the Black Arts Movement. This was important because always one of the characteristic features of social transformation is that it is expressed very clearly in the struggling peoples' artistic culture. So during the most intense period of the BLM, the Black Arts Movement spoke with the same fire, drawn from the same Black hearts.

At the Arts, Yusef played Clay in *Dutchman*, an armed Black militant in Charles Patterson's *Black Ice* and in my own *Experimental Death Unit #1*. He was part of that Black Arts Repertory Theater company that moved from site to site, from playground to sidewalk to park to vacant lot all summer (1965) as we staged plays, had showings of Black painters' works, read poetry, brought the newest of our music into the streets as part of the HarYou summer program ("Operation Boot Strap" . . . indeed!) We created a Black Arts' Summer! Moving a multifaceted Black and extremely militant arts program all over Harlem.

Later, Yusef came to Newark as part of the *Spirit House Movers*, our continuing Black Arts theater group in Newark. (Along with his wire, Doris, their children, plus his sister Truly, his brother, Justice, the whole family.)

He was a new kinda Rochester in *JELLO*: the wise black magician, Nasafi, in Black Mass, trying to stop the mad Yacub from creating Bernhard Goetz ("Yacub, this thing has no human soul!"). He was the dancing and enlightened robber in *Home On*

The Range and the second story man who gets to play God in *The First Militant Preacher*, Ben Caldwell's Black militant satire that traveled halfway around the world. ("I can do anything but fail!")

Yusef did multiple roles in a rush of new plays the period brought out. In each period of Black political upsurge there is also a period of Black artistic upsurge. And more than anything, Yusef Iman was a revolutionary.

Like the host of us young people then to embrace the Black Arts Movement, we were Black Revolutionaries **1st**—our art was our weapon. We wanted art that was identifiably **Afro-American, mass oriented**, and **revolutionary**.

Yusef was one of the original Spirit House Movers and also among that group of poets who went from city to city, bringing the message of Black Art: Black Revolution (WE NEED IT NOW!). He was an unrelenting word warrior in his poetry. "White White White White White White White ahhhhhhh, NO wonder I hate Myself!" Yusef said, satirizing the truly sick Negro, like those jurors on the Goetz case.

He said in another poem, *Love Yr Enemy*, "Love, Love, Love, Love . . . Love / For everybody else. / But When will we Love / Our selves?"

When he traveled and worked with the acting company he was equally unbridled, fiery, dynamic, energetic, unrelenting and militant, yes, always, Black & Militant! Of all the people I knew and worked with as an artist, Yusef, to me, was the classic, the most mass confirmed version of the Black revolutionary "nightmare" that exploded in the '60s in the U.S.; one of the towering figures who threw racist U.S. culture into a fright and frenzy, just by showing Black life fighting to survive the pre-human reign of the white supremacy monsters.

Yusef burned imperialism's butt nightly somewhere in America during that time. That's what made him happiest, "Burning the Devil!" He read poems, acted, sang, even danced. When he played the junk wasted straw boss pusher for the mob in *Junkies Are Full of Shhhh*, an enraged sister started to beat on Yusef one evening as we finished, convinced he was the real "Doo Doo"!

Yusef was in the world premiere performances of *Slave Ship* at the Spirit House. He is featured with myself, Doris, Freddie Johnson and the Jihad Singers on *Black & Beautiful, Soul & Madness*, the poetry and R&B record we made in 1968.

He bellows Nasafi's warnings on the record of *Black Mass* above the sprawling chilling satanic atmospheric music of the great Sun Ra, begging us not to create things in human form who have no feeling for human life. (Now we have 666 as president, just as *The Omen* said.)

The grinning Tom in *Slave Ship*, as well as the African warrior resisting slavery, Yusef Iman expressed a wide range of indelible portraits. The worker in *"What Was the Relationship of the Lone Ranger to the Means of Production?"*

Yusef's death should stop us in our tracks and give us the deepest caution. first, because too many of us, too many people close to us, people who were central strong figures in the '60s, are dying. Even while we grieve, let us be ever-vigilant!!!

We know what Yusef would say about Howard Beach or Forsythe County or the Goetz case. I can already see a play with Yusef as Roy Innis on the train in a Goetz situation, but also Yusef as one of the tragic young brothers tricked inside by white supremacy. Amina, Furaha, Mchochezi, Jaribu, Ngoma, and some others, would be in it too.

Yusef's passing is so staggering and so thought provoking because even though we are in a dangerous right wing period, up under the gun of the killer-fool, Chief Klansman Reagan, there are signs that we might be ready to move again. That we've had enough of this most recent rightward surge, this time directly toward **Fascism**.

Israel in the north, Boers in the south, cap Mother Africa and the Arab world with chains, continuing to pillage and loot Mother Africa, whose riches are still used to enslave us because they are not controlled by the people.

Yusef, like those of us who chose to give our principal energies to opposing and one day destroying white supremacy and imperialism, knew that our slavery in the U.S. is linked to the subjugation of Black people and colored people worldwide. I know he would welcome the signs of new militancy, springing up in diverse places.

Yusef would shake his head and chuckle bitterly about the backward Negro, "Brother, Brother, Brother," he'd say, "What we gonna do with our people?"

The Klan is screaming recruitment in Queens, now that they have made it legal to kill Black youth. Yusef was in a play in 1967 called *Arm Yrself or Harm Yrself* at Spirit House and touring. We have to bring it back!

That information seems much needed again today. Especially since now we know if we are confronted by people we feel are hostile to us we can shoot them down. Yusef could talk badder about "The Devil" than anyone I ever heard. Devil, Klansmen, animalistic Americans like the ones at Howard Beach or Forsythe County, or the ones in blue like the savage murderers of Claude Reese or Louis Baez or Arthur Miller or Michael Stewart .

"Brother, You better Arm Yrself Or Harm Yrself," Yusef would say in his wild Black-Up style. "Brotha, Sista, You betta Arm Yourself or Harm Your Self".

Hey, Brother, NDUGU, We hear you! We hear you!

Tutaonana,
Pamoja Tutashinda!

1987

Al White (1937-1984)

Eulogy For Al White

Life sometimes is so seemingly purposeless and bizarre that we are never really reconciled to it. We seek refuge in fantasy because Life will give no easy answers or pat solutions.

But for those who in despair might cry out, "What is the meaning of life?" As some of us here might, especially if we are close to the bereaved family, particularly to the surviving daughter and sister, Alberta. Al White's life might give a clue.

In a few brief months, we have seen almost an entire family disappear and be no more. A father and two sons. A few years before that, the beloved mother.

"What is the purpose of Life?" we cry, our sorrow seemingly interminable. "What are we living for?" But the answer is obvious. Life is its own purpose.

Al White (and all the Whites) seemed to know that. Not only that life is its own purpose but its own reward.

I first met Allan around downtown New York, what's called Greenwich Village, during the vanished '50s. We were both swift young men, linked by friendship with another young Jerseyan, Allen Polite.

Polite had come to The Village earlier than Allan and I. His Bedford St. apartment was our beachhead in the big time downtown Bohemian world.

Allan White had many interests and they changed from time to time. But what was constant about Allan White was that he knew life is its own reward. Because Al was alive when we was. He was not half stepping. He tried to live his life to the hilt.

Al loved music and trumpet immortal, Miles Davis, was one of his special friends. Al had the sensibility of an artist. And for a time, Al pursued sculpting. Even recently I talked to Al one night in New York's *Sweet Basil*, he was talking about how he had just finished "studying silver."

But quite a few years ago, Al moved into cosmetology and hair design, becoming a beautician just as his mother was. He worked in NYC shops for a time and then finally he returned to Jersey to work with his mother in her shop. It was during this period that Al became associated with the *Ebony Fashion Fair* and their annual tour.

He also began to work as a hair designer in various Broadway productions. Particularly memorable was his work in the Broadway play *I Do I Do* with Mary Martin and Robert Preston. Al also worked with Diana Sands when she did *St. Joan*, as well as the Johnny Carson show.

Al also went to the Clairol School of Coloring as a result of which he was sent to Brussels, Belgium for nine months. Later, he opened two beauty shops in New Jersey, *The Magic Comb* in East Orange and *The Impulse Salon* on Halsey St. in Newark.

Eventually Al moved back to "The City" and was a well known figure living in NYC's Greenwich Village.

In the last years Al had grown increasingly interested in antiques and handicrafts, like his elder brother Tom. He also still maintained his connection with the theater and films through frequent bit parts.

Allen was a consumate raconteur and bon vivant. He was an elegant dresser, a bit of a romantic with the same good looks that characterized his family. And as I said from the outset, Al White knew how to live, and he knew living was life's most wonderful priority.

I saw Al just a few days before he died. Naturally, in "The Village" where both our young minds had been turned on earlier to the cosmopolitan and the aesthetic. He was trying to get me to come to an affair introducing a cousin of his who was running for mayor over in Jersey. (John Hatcher, who subsequently won that election.) That was the latest and perhaps the last of Al's many passions. But knowing Al put one in closer proximity to life itself. Because that's what Al was about . . . Life and The Living of it! We'll miss him alright.

1984

Tom White (1935-1984)

Tom White—Business Man

A generation is like a wave, suddenly, yet predictably, rushing in. It's great power. It's awesome size. It's fantastic sound!

Each of us come here as part of specific new generations,who met their challenges, grew past childhood, and either fulfilled generally heroic lives, no matter the pain & tragedy, or else we are the failed, who are constantly condemned, even by our selves.

I am of the same generation, as many of you are, of the dead brother here. Some of you are of other generations, younger, older, but you are here as different parts of the whole.

Our lives are special and magnificent and the sweetest aspect of that is knowledge, good friends and a good record! The whole world is like us, except we know each other.

The Black "Race" is emerging from worldwide persecution and slavery. We are among the most democratic and revolutionary people, because we are still fighting for our **own** freedom! Our slaughter and renaissances have made us good at running and hitting people.

The most useful of us are trying to understand how to make our lives, together, more fulfilling and more full of consciousness. Our consciousness ties us to people who also thirst and hunger after freedom. There is a communication between us that draws us to each other to try to transform this narrow society.

The Jazz Art Music Society in Newark used Black culture to raise people's consciousness. Afro conscious, Art inspired, Jazz-animated. My wife Amina, was also one of the movers in the Jazz Art Society. And Tom was always one of the movers and shakers. Some of the projects Tom was associated with:

—**1962 Muslim Bazaar** (Tom was an early supporter of the Nation of Islam for their economic and political lines. Even when it wasn't generally popular with mainstream Black business)

—**World Wide Handicrafts** (one of the first Black stores to give us access to arts and crafts of the world)

—**Black Business** (Tom was a stalwart, from the beginning pushing "do for self." And then doing it. He saw Black business as a means to self determination!)

—**Black Culture & Art** (Tom knew the relationship between Black culture and art and Black social development and self-determination)

—**African Culture & Art** (Tom had a Pan-Africanist sense, in that he felt that African peoples' fate, all over the world, was inevitably bound together. And that, indeed, Afro-Americans **were** "an African people.")

". . . [F]rom merely consumers to entrepreneurs, manufacturers and producers . . . they will then be self educators. Malcolm, especially after Mecca. Du Bois, Douglass, J.A. Rogers, taught that."

This was the way Tom White saw it. And pushed it from his *World Wide Handicrafts*. Reaching out to the Third World and the emerging peoples.

In 1970, he was one of the Black businessmen who backed Ken Gibson for mayor. From there he put together the 72 Halsey St. Association and proposed a mall on Halsey St.

I know it will be hard for Tom to rest in peace until we have removed all barriers in our way to full human life and expression. Tom realized we had got rid of the sheriff. What he and me and we want to know, still, is how do you get rid of the deputy? Rest, soon, Tom!

1984

"Philly" Joe Jones (1923-1985)

The Pause of Joe

                    Philly Joe Jones
                         Joseph Jones
                              of Philly
Arc of bones
        on board
             in the sea's darkness
                    being bones
        of the being beaten

                         of the Joes
                              the eyes
                         of the sleekest
                    thou seekest our injury
                    Being
                              Us

                         & the bones beat
                              beat out

                         as the drums are
                         a form of space

                         its life containing
        Whatever must exist
        trace
        flight
        flame

        these years of times lasso
             the cross eyed deity
                    of laughter
                         beat bones

        *   *   *
    tell the blood
        the Blood's
              story

             His
                  story

    The Beat of Joe
        I eye
    the Kansas city 4 man
    came on Winged Feet
        Thats yr Papa
            Eye Eye
    A Spanish guy
    The story teller

    Jo Jo

    Story telling bones
    Blood
        Stones
        Death
        & Life
        Tones
                        Tell The Story Joe
                        Eye Story
                              Yo Man
                              Jo Man

As yr beaten lives and grows
the grapevine of the world serpent
shakes, Tell the Story Joe

We're no grimace
    in this menace
    as if minutes

    this telling

blow
Joe

For darkness, under sea lingo
              tengo
              mucho
          story we
          no can say

     Let bones beat it
          take the air
          above the trees
          a herd of me's

     Tell the Story
     Joe
     Philly Dilly
          Bone speech

                              Sleek

of the Dead Seek
     Bones Speak

                         Griot
                         Story Teller
                    From Philadelphia
                Which DuBois Analyzed

                    Found The Negroes
                         Wise
                    & Thriving On A Riff
               Thriving beneath the Veil
               This Century's Jail
                         Yee Slave Folk
                         & Masters
               Yee Magic Cans
                    of the Streets
                         & thrilling ghettos
                    Where the Slums
               beat like a boom a loom

                                        Cage
                              for the Africans
                                    to beat out
                                      their age
                              to let out their
                                        Rage
                                     Be a Bone
                                  & Speak, Joe

                                 You & He from Kansas
                                         City
                                   The Four-Man
                        & Bats' Kin He mimics
                                    to teach us
                                    In Omen Land
                                     The Count
                                  Processed In Funk
                             Some Monkish Draculaics
                          For the visiting Klan, The Bone
                                    Beats
                                    Hides
                                    Speak
                       This Political Tongue
                         Speech of Marches
                         The Black
                         Fire Men
              Their Sirens Tell of Escapes
            Joe Griot dusts his iron tales
       the metal sings industrial Blues
          Machine Funk.

       You wd have to be hip
          to be w/ Miles
             So Bad
             Was He
          This King of MaMa Rappers
             Black Sweet Swift

reflections of night
in his shining hair

                    I was there
                    The Music in his stare

of Philly-ness
 & Joe-ness
 & for Eloise even
    Joseph-ness
 The Lone Star
 above the
      rhythm House.

                    We said
                              Miles & Trane
                              & Philly
                              & Them
                    (that's Paul & Red
                    & Blue Cannon Ball
                    Fusing The Master Classic
                                        Bop-Cool

 & Harder Bopper
School

                              The State of the Art
                    For those who came to play
                              The Heart's
                              Message

For Bravery
For Philadelphia Jokes
For such gladness
    as only a friend
    can give
    or know
    or be
Free as his Shakerei
        brushes
  Mississippi Sound

Joseph The Father

Max The Son
Joseph The Holy
      Philadelphia
      Ghost
& Klook be they
Bop

As our hearts
locked in sun

Tell the history

Like Joe & I
& Archie
one night

What Bad Tadd said
  Philly JJ

  The Bones Song
  Dameronia

So we knew Joe to speak
      Yo can seek
      We the see
      Bop the Be

    Free Joe
His style as form's
  essence
  yet the rumble

  the reach
  beneath black seas

  to rail roads of ebony
  skeletons

on the way to Slavery
                land
Us Congos
held by a
Square
        Joe
    was there

Mr. Jones
        Mr. Joseph Rudolf Jones
        from Philadelphia
So bad a city
took his name
& so its fame
despite those evil servants

of 666
who have
come
to
No Goode!

He breathed our history as
his walking beat

Bones & Hide
  Shimmering
    metal
        strut.

Dixie Peach
        2/4
        Napoleon
    We copped
        yr band
        for coming

        against our will

        Toussaint
& Christophe
& Sidney Bechet
copped
took it wherever other
bone sings
      sun
            hide
                  beats

      the niggers
      of the orchestra   sd Max

      quite
      naturally
                        Yo, man
                                          Joe,
                                                can

You wd have to be hip to
                  hang out
                  w/ Miles
                  & Trane
      To have a city
      use yr
      name

To get the bones
to beat its name

Brothers
Do Love

& Negroes be here
   too

& Crazy Benjamin
out there

70

messin
w/ that
electricity
"Boy, you better
come up
out the rain
w/ that
key!!

Try See, Yo
          Jo
     about here
Africa
The South
New Orleans
          Blue
Spanish Tinge
City Rock
Miles Stones
Funky Blues

On A Misty Night, Lady Bird
The Bones
Speak
of Rag & Swing
     & Boogie

     of March
     & Colored Ghosts

Ashé Ashé
Guanguanco
Signifying Elegba
God of Laughter & *Jasm*

Beater of Bones & Hides
Singer w/ Golden Symbols
          Bop Be

Be
Thy Name

Domesticater of Animals
Master of the Fields & Flowering Seeds
Builder of Houses in One Place
Keeper of the Herds

Speaker of a thousand tongues
    some as swift
    as the wind

  City Man
Collector of Art
    & culture
    Creator of Museums
            & Libraries

    Civilizer
    of the Dark

    Introducer
    of the *Human*
    Being

Poet of Industrial Design
Machine Singer

Language Maker
  Song & Dance
  Man

        Yo
    there is no
        Urban
        No post-desert
        Science
    w/o yr tom toms

& shades
        Yo, Jo
    I & I
& The Four-Man now also gone

So we who remain
    who know the game
    who have seen slavery
    give way to the Gestapo

    & see the slow worm
    of fascism

    pop out
    Reagan headed

    from a cancerous
    nose

Those of us who do
    knows

        That Duke & Count
        & John Before
        & Pres & Louie
        & then Thelonius

        & before two suns
        Both the Father
        & the Ghost

How much strength
is our history

How much Beauty
& Dancing

How much struggle

is our memory

Our Dream of
    Democracy

Bone Man
Beat Darkness
        into Singing
                    Sun

        into Colored
                    Rhythms

        Against the
        Boers

        & No Goodes

        A hipper time than
        Pendulums

        much clearer
        than Clarence

Let it Be Known Now that you
        Carriers of the
        Torch
        of the Created
                        Advancing
                        Mind

That throughout this world
        Huge Changes Ready
            to go
            Down

            From the top

Let the baton of rhythms
        of riddims
        of Rap
        Reggae
of the Sorrow Songs

The hide & rock
        roll & beat
                shimmer of street

                tough growling
                shaded
                Orisha of
        Bop Bee

They say in prayer to the living
        now & forever
        Our Jasm
                Creators
                in life
        of its hearts
                essence

        It's on you   (now
                                                it's on
        they say: you)

All our history

        Slavery &
        Ghosts
Maniac Kings
Who sold us in chains

For Duke & Monk
   & John & Thelonius
   & Yo, double Joe

The Father
& the Wholly Philadelphia
        Ghost

They're Here-ing
is a hum of old grandmothers
a hum of deacons
a hum of Lindy Hopping Rappers
of Cake Walkers
Tappers, Yo, Jo
        I Know
You had to go
This slow poison world
Cdn't handle you

Yet your hear-ing
        is your bone
                        beat
                hide under
                hand &
                stick

        the riddim say
        It's On You

        rookieeeeeeeeeeeee
        Do Bana Coba
        Do Bana Coba   Beneme   Beneme

I heard my man the other day
        Joe Say

        Beating the telling
                Bones
        Yo, Rookie
        Yng blood

                                        Nation to Be

Bigging People   Rising to We
                                   Free Nation
of a Vision   To See
a riddim
a desire
            a fire
of human science
            love a beat
            a heart

      says:
            Its on you

            on you now
                  on you

This Music
      of our world's
            Description

      Hymn For The As We wd
      Say Him
            Self
            One of
The Great
      MaMa Lamas

The Man
So Hip
A City
Took
His
                  Name!!

PHILADELPHIA JOE JONES

                              1985

77

G. L. ("George") Russ (1902-1983)

G. L. "George" Russ
December 28, 1902 - January 17, 1983

G. L. Russ was born in Dothan, Alabama, just after the turn of the century, to Thomas Everett and Anna Belle Russ. G. L. came up with the name George a little later, when folks thought that the old southern tradition of naming people with initials wouldn't do, so G. L. became, in a few years, George. Though, people in the family mostly called him G. L. or just G.

G. L. was the brother of Mrs. Anna Lois Jones. He went to school, during the early grammar school years, in Dothan. He also helped his father out in the grocery stores and funeral parlor that Thomas Russ was proprietor of in Dothan, before racist forces destroyed these businesses and the Russes had to move north, like so many other black people during that period.

The family moved to Beaver Falls, Pennsylvania, and here, G. L., now supposedly George, went to Beaver Falls Public School and later Lynchburg Bible School. The family and G. L. were also affiliated in Beaver Falls with the 24th St. Baptist Church and the Tabernacle Baptist Church. And once the family moved to Newark, in 1926, G, along with the rest of the family, became affiliated with Bethany Baptist Church, in which they still are.

George Russ was employed by his father Thomas Russ, until the Depression ended the elder Russ's grocery business. George later worked with Horn and Hardart, Philadelphia; for a long time as a Pullman Porter with the Pennsylvania Railroad; and later with Unity Life Insurance Co. and McGraw Hill Publishers, New York.

G. L. was always a very active person and always on the go. He was, for a long time, the classic "man about town," like his father, interested in politics and social life, as well as church affairs. G. L.

was a very sophisticated and well-read man and he always served as a vital source of information and inspiration for his sister's children, when the Russes and Joneses were growing up together. His niece, Sandra Elaine Jones, also known as Kimako Baraka, and his nephew Everett LeRoi Jones, also known as Amiri Baraka, sat many years at G. L.'s feet absorbing his sophisticated analysis of the world.

No one ever believes in death; and when it comes, they believe it even less! For one thing, the family cannot believe G. L. is gone. He of the deep voice and the ready word. He who never accepted adversity or ignorance but always thought, and demonstrated with this life, that no matter how hard somebody might try, that they couldn't keep him or us down. G. L.'s was such a positive spirit, so much a part of the world, yet always looking to transcend it.

The family remembers how his mother, Nana, when she wanted to call any of us, would start with G. L. and say "G". "Lo", "Lee", "Laine", meaning G. L., Lois, LeRoi, Elaine; she had to go through the entire catalog to get to any one of us, mothers and children, uncles and nephews. And for the nieces and nephews, and now the grand nieces and nephews, they will always remember "Uncle." The word was so impacted with love and respect that the entire family, regardless of their relationship, called George Russ "Uncle" as if there was only one person in the world who carried that title, "Uncle." Even his sister and brother-in-law finally called him that, "Uncle," which did symbolize his relationship to the whole family. Our "Uncle," some wise and urbane figure we would call on when we needed to know for sure. When we needed some backup, some warmth and love. Now "Uncle" is gone, but the family will not admit it. You see, "No one ever believes in death; and when it comes, they believe it even less." But goodbye, "Uncle". Take care of yourself. We'll meet again, some way!!

1983

Bob Kaufman (1925-1986)

A Meditation on Bob Kaufman

Frink   /
    /   Kauf meant thought
Banged
Back

  in A L T I T U D E

So that thought
  & "Freak"
      collided

    to
    HANG

    City Side

    Quiet as

    breathing

Always
  Frinking

    ABOMUNISTS

    WERE

    UNDERCOVER

    HUMANS

LAUGHING

FOOT PRINTS

–

BOB KNEW VIOLENCE
REMEMBERED
HIS HAIR

& FRINK

SUSPECTED
HE RODE AS
WELL AS
WORSHIPPED
Pterodactyls

He knew the
poison
equation

Dorsey
Rothschild
(TIME)
SMOKE

MINE
vs
(RHYTHM)
o   o
o   o
o   o

81

```
o        o
o        o
o        o
o        o
D E A T H
   oo
```

WOLFMAN

WOLFMAN

Pterodactyls
WING THUMP SHADOW
   Across   Earth

BOP

CRACKLE ELECTRICITY TO
   BE
ATOMIC PERSONAL DOT
ABOMUNIST PRINTS
1ST AMENDMENT
   FRANKENSTEIN
CAVE HIPSTER
1ST COOKER AMIDST
Red Dripping Teeth
Mad Animal Family
Hoppers Opposition
Up top the tree
Bob roosted to see

the stars, Atomic television
sky, life itself,
hairy astrologer communist
the big feet
tracking across the

Be
Bomkauf, from his
Sightings
his hip sat thought
time pattern
was called
said the correct
          path
     the right
       way
     the print
     is what stooges
     say is an
empty   foot

     Ark

Hairy half person

     to whom

     they never

       ain't

Any way!

     Hence *Bop*,
the triumph of clubs
          as
          trumps.

Donald like his Duck
          A Quack
& not a rise
his pitiful paper
& shiny metal
          personality

* * *

& Trump is not Jewish
or You/ish (except
when you are
gaseous)
a lowered
the same as Lord

in dispense wit
the whole height of
site's sight. We stay up
all night, dont fight,
create & dig light.

And then the egg man
wants humans & sees
print & bans it.

———————

Wolf man over Wolf man

———————

All nation's equation
The Base, de base
so now its crackers
before it was jigs
our hairy mamas
did the work and
farther on the hype.

Scuse me tracks, BombKauf
isolated in West Jaws
a trick story (some say)
others
opportunize around
his myth

Sons & Lovers
Boiled yeggs & ohs
Seeds of non dick howling
crime pee

My friend drama town
City lights will cook
the boy
his head, shorn, his smile,
worn

For we who have never been
    anarchists
        who have never been
        Buddhists
        Us Sheeps
        of Storm Center

"Lover" is one of Jimmy's
    Brothers'
names. Get to that!
At my worst I was a King
& turned President
as a resident

Now the clouds
    wave me
        back
         or
        Black

I cant Attack
    No Real
        Life
A Stooge
    is Eating
the Pop Corn
    Joey.

This is our only noise
       & its a song
             on television

I say BombKauf, the
             ABomunists
Were
Reds
whose foot prints yodeled
like pre God Pygmies

BombKauf
    you were an egg beater
        no ego
        but the closing eye

        of slipping

        nigger death

(to the whiteness which
    Keeps his memory

      a Fish
      a Cross
      a Furnace of Evil
       A Growed up Nazi to be
        Full fledged
            White Guy!

The abominable
    snowman

nasty
coke
in
Athens

Where
Everything, even
Water
Melons

was Created

Human
Beings
Bob
That's what you
Heard

A POST AMERICAN

Phenomenon

Communists
are the
ones

Tracked down
By
No Man

No Oh

S'NO MAN'S
NOR WOMAN'S
HEAR?
(This place

                    Race itself spells
                    Competition
                         19th century

All the way

& then they even lost

that!

        Over the hill to
        Grandma's house
        Over the sea's to
        we nother better hip

        you dig?
Abomunist
            try
Communist

Await on skates, post the
        dead dug
Lightning
Fast, no meat
            meeting

        Knew
        then
        New
      No Sin
Being What All
        of it
        & Any
        Plenty
my man, us
all men
& Them w/ Wombs

we working
on that

It's Why the Sun

    Do
What It
    Do

    We don't recognize

    Anything

    Unless

    We're gone
        be recognized
      in that messy
            manner

A live Shadow farting
   like a
   brain
   clock
O? Aha? Yes!

No Know
It's all here going away,
     waving
        pictures
      breathing
      pictures
      imagining
      pictures
      live feeling. Bob

Round up voices, bodies
& flicks

*   *   *

Every All wants & wents
                                to
    be   No Shit

    That's the only rule
& of course I'm going
to the bath room
    in a lidda
        while

PAST US

US PAST

NEVER

&c

EVER

&c

            Why dont we turn

            around?

            The usual suspects

            Hoo   Ray!

            Hoo   Ray!

                                        1991

James Arthur Baldwin (1924-1987)

Jimmy!

We know, or ought to know by now, that what we call "reality" exists independent of any of the multivisioned subjectivisms that nevertheless distort and actually peril all life here. For me, one clear example of the dichotomy between what actually is and what might be reflected in some smeared mirror of private need, is the public characterization of the mighty being for whom we are gathered here to bid our tearful farewells!

You will notice, happily, or with whatever degree of predictable social confusion, that I have spoken of *Jimmy*. And it is he, this Jimmy, of whom I will continue to speak. It is this Jimmy, this glorious, elegant griot of our oppressed African American nation who I am eulogizing. So let the butchering copy editors of our captivity stay for an eternal moment their dead eraser fingers from our celebration.

There will be, and should be, reams and reams of analysis, even praise, for our friend but also even larger measures of non-analysis and certainly condemnation for James Baldwin, the Negro writer. Alas we have not yet the power to render completely sterile or make impossible the errors and lies which will merely be America being itself rather than its unconvincing promise.

But the wide gap, the world spanning abyss, between the James Baldwin of yellow journalism and English departments (and here we thought this was America), and the Jimmy Baldwin of our real lives, is stunning! When he told us *Nobody Knows My* (he meant Our) *Name*, he was trying to get you ready for it even then!

For one thing, no matter the piles of deathly prose citing influences, relationships, metaphor and criticism that will attempt to tell us about our older brother, most will miss the mark, simply because for the most part they will be retelling old lies or making up new ones, or shaping yet another black life to fit the great white stomach which yet rules and tries to digest the world!

For first of all Jimmy Baldwin was not only a writer, an international literary figure, he was man, spirit, voice—old and black and terrible as that first ancestor.

As man, he came to us from the family, the human lives, names we can call David, Gloria, Lover, Robert . . . and this extension, is one intimate identification as he could so casually, in that way of his, eyes and self smiling, not much larger than that first ancestor, fragile as truth always is, big eyes popped out like righteous monitors of the soulful. The Africans say that big ol' eyes like that means someone can make things happen! And didn't he?

Between Jimmy's smile and grace, his insistent elegance even as he damned you, even as he smote what evil was unfortunate, breathing or otherwise, to stumble his way. He was all the way live, all the way conscious, turned all the way up, receiving and broadcasting, sometime so hard, what needed to, would back up from those two television tubes poking out of his head!

As man, he was my friend, my older brother he would joke, not really joking. As man he was Our friend, Our older or younger brother. We listened to him like we would somebody in our family, whatever you might think of what he might say. We could hear it. He was close, as man, as human relative, we could make it some cold seasons merely warmed by his handshake, smile or eyes. Warmed by his voice, jocular yet instantly cutting. Kind yet perfectly clear. We could make it sometimes, just remembering his arm waved in confirmation or indignation, the rapid fire speech, pushing out at the world like urgent messages for those who would be real.

This man traveled the earth like its history and its biographer. He reported, criticized, made beautiful, analyzed, cajoled, lyricized, attacked, sang, made us better, made us consciously human or perhaps more acidly pre-human.

He was spirit because he was living. And even past this tragic hour when we weep he has gone away, and why, and why we keep asking. There's mountains of evil creatures who we would willingly bid farewell to—Jimmy could have given you some of their names on demand—We curse our luck, our oppressors—our age, our weakness. Why & Why again? And why can drive you mad, or said enough times might even make you wise!

Yet this *why* in us is in him as well. Jimmy was wise from asking whys giving us his wise and his whys to go with our own, to make them into a larger why and a deeper Wise.

Jimmy's spirit, which will be with us as long as we remember ourselves, is the only truth which keeps us sane and changes our whys to wiseness. It is his spirit, spirit of the little black first ancestor, which we feel, those of us who really felt it, we know this spirit will be with us for "as long as the sun shines and the water flows." For his is the spirit of life thrilling to its own consciousness.

His spirit is part of our own, it is our feelings' completion. Our perceptions' extension, the edge of our rationale, the paradigm for our best use of this world.

When we saw and heard him, he made us feel good. He made us feel, for one thing, that we could defend ourselves and define ourselves, that we were in the world not merely as animate slaves, but as terrifyingly sensitive measurers of what is good or evil, beautiful or ugly. This is the power of his spirit. This is the bond which created our love for him. This is the fire that terrifies our pitiful enemies. That not only are we alive but shatteringly precise in our songs and our scorn. You could not possibly think yourself righteous, Murderers, when you saw or were wrenched by our Jimmy's spirit! He was carrying it as us, as we carry him as us.

Jimmy will be remembered, even as James, for his word. Only the completely ignorant can doubt his mastery of it. Jimmy Baldwin was the creator of contemporary American speech even before Americans could dig that. He created it so we could speak to each other at unimaginable intensities of feeling, so we could make sense to each other at yet higher and higher tempos.

But that word, arranged as art, sparkling and gesturing from the page, was also man and spirit. Nothing was more inspiring than hearing that voice, seeing that face, and that whip of tongue, that signification that was his fingers, reveal and expose, raise and bring down, condemn or extol!

I had met him years before at Howard, when Owen Dodson presented his *Amen Corner* there. But it was not until later, confined by the armed forces, that I got to feel that spirit from another more desperate angle of need, and therefore understanding.

Jimmy's face, his eyes, the flush of his consciousness animating the breath of my mind, sprung from my earlier reading of his early efforts in literary magazines, and the aura those efforts created, stretched itself, awakened so to speak, when I stared—newly arrived in New York from my imprisonment and internal confusion—to see this black man staring from the cover of *Notes of a Native Son* at me unblinking. I looked at that face, and heard that voice, even before I read the book. Hey, it was me, for real! When I read those marvelous essays, that voice became part of my life forever. Those eyes were part of my instruments of judgment and determination. Those deliberations, that experience, the grimness and high art, became mine instantly. From the moment I saw his face, he was my deepest hero, the agent of consciousness in my young life. Jimmy was that for many of us.

What was said of him, the so-called analysis, often reeking of the dead smell of white supremacy and its non-existent humanity, made no difference. All of that did not really register, except as recall for dull conversations with fire plugs or chairs or stone steps when abroad in the practiced indifference called U.S. society.

What he gave me, what he gave us, we perceived instantly and grew enormous inside because of it. That black warm truth. That invincible gesture of sacred human concern, clearly projected, we absorbed with what gives life in this world contrasted as it is against the dangerous powers of death.

Jimmy grew as we all did, but he was growing first and was the measure, even as we claimed understanding and transcendence. Just as he wanted to distance himself from a mentor like Richard Wright, better to understand more clearly where he himself, his own self and voice began and Richard's left off.

Happily for some of us, when we distanced ourselves from Jimmy, it turned out that this not only let us understand ourselves more clearly, but it allowed us finally to come to grips with the actual truth power and beauty of this artist and hero.

It was Jimmy who led us from Critical Realism to an aesthetic furthering of it that made it more useful to the still living. He was like us so much, constantly growing, constantly measuring himself against himself, and thus against the world.

It was evident he loved beauty and art, but when the Civil Rights Movement pitched to its height, no matter his early aestheticism and seeming hauteur, he was our truest definer, our educated conscience made irresistible by his high consciousness.

Jimmy was a "civil rights leader" too, *at the same time*!, thinkers of outmoded social outrage. He was in the truest tradition of the great artists of all times. Those who understand it is *beauty and truth* we seek, and that indeed one cannot exist without and as an extension of the other.

At the hot peak of the movement Jimmy was one of its truest voices. His stance, that it is *our judgment* of the world, the majority of us who still struggle to survive the bestiality of so called civilization, (the slaves) that is true and not that of our torturers, was a dangerous profundity and, as such, fuel for our getaway and liberation!

He was our consummate & complete man of letters, not as an unliving artifact, but as a black man we could touch and relate to even there in that space filled with black fire at the base and circumference of our souls. And what was supremely ironic is that for all his aestheticism and ultra-sophistication, there he was now demanding that we get in the world completely, that we comprehend the ultimate intelligence of our enforced commitment to finally bring humanity to the world!

Jimmy's voice, as much as Dr. King's or Malcolm X's, helped shepherd and guide us toward black liberation.

And for this, of course, the intellectual gunmen of the animal king tried to vanquish him. For ultimately, even the rare lyricism of his song, the sweeping aesthetic obsession with feeling, could not cover the social heaviness of his communication!

The celebrated James Baldwin of earlier times could not be used to cover the undaunted freedom chants of the Jimmy who walked with King and SNCC or the evil little nigger who wrote *Blues For Mr. Charlie*!

For as far as I'm concerned, it was *Blues For Mr. Charlie* that announced the Black Arts Movement, even so far as describing down to minute fragments of breath, the class struggle raging inside the black community. Even as it is menaced by prehuman maniacs.

But attacked or not, repressed or not, suddenly un-newsworthy or not, Jimmy did what Jimmy was. He lived his life as witness. He wrote until the end. We hear of the writers' blocks of celebrated Americans, how great they are so great indeed that their writing fingers have been turned to checks, but Jimmy wrote. He produced. He spoke. He sang, no matter the odds. He remained man, and spirit and voice. Ever-expanding, ever-more-conscious!

Gratifying to me in the extreme was that each year we grew closer, grew to understand each other even more. Ultimately I did understand, as I feel I always did, but now consciously, that he was my older brother, a brother of the communal spirit!!

One day I took him to Newark's Scudder Homes, the toilet bowl of the world, with a film crew. Seemingly deserted at first, the streets, once the vine got to graping, filled quickly and Jimmy found himself surrounded by black people eager only to look at him, ask him questions, or tell him he was still their main man. At that nadir of social dislocation, one young brother his hat turned half way around said, "I just read *Just Above My Head*, Mr. Baldwin. It's great! How you doing?" Jimmy's smile of recognition alone would have lit up even the darker regions under the earth.

We hung out all night one time lurching out of Mikell's after talking to David, and the next morning, Jimmy still leading and gesturing, clear as a bell, was still telling me some things I really needed to know, and I was still giving him feedback that yes there were a bunch of us who knew who he was, and loved him for it, since it was one of the only ways we could ever really love ourselves!! Jimmy was one of those people whose celebrity is recognized whether by name or not, by the very aura that accompanied him. Whose intelligence is revealed in the most casual gesture or turn of apparel and bearing. We were aware at once that such dignity was the basis and result of great achievement of serious regard for the deep, the heavy, the profound.

Yet, because of this deep and deeply felt by us integrity Jimmy carried like his many hats, his film of *Malcolm X* was rejected, reviews of his later works began to appear on page two, because he could not be permitted to tell the truth so forcefully. Finally, great minds even forbade him to publish his last work, *The Evidence of Things Not Seen*, exposing the duplicity of the legal machinations obscuring the real killers of the black Atlanta children. He had to sue the publisher in order to get the book out! When he told me this last outrage, I remember the word *Weimar* flashed through my head. Reading this formidable completely mature and awesome work, I could understand the terror of White Supremacy and its worshippers, at its appearance. It is important that I include this quote from the work as his man, spirit voice, flesh of his soul speaking to us with the clarity of revelation:

> *The Western world is located somewhere between the Statue of Liberty and the pillar of salt.*
>
> *At the center of the European horror is their religion: a religion by which it is intended one be coerced, and in which no one believes, the proof being the Black/White conditions, or options, the horror into which the cowardly delusion of White supremacy seems to have transformed Africa, and the utterly intolerable nightmare of the American Dream. I speak with the authority of the grandson of a slave, issue of the bondswoman, Hagar's child. And, what the slave did— despised and rejected, 'buked and scorned with the European's paranoid vision of human life was to alchemize it into a force that contained a human use. The Black preacher, since the church was the only Civilized institution that we were permitted—separately—to enter, was our first warrior, terrorist, or guerrilla. He said that freedom was real—that we were real. He told us that trouble don't last always. He told us that our children and our elders were sacred, when the Civilized were spitting on them and hacking them to*

pieces, in the name of God, and in order to keep on making money. And, furthermore, we were not so much permitted to enter the church as corralled into it, as a means of rendering us docile and as a means of forcing us to corroborate the inscrutable will of God, Who had decreed that we should be slaves forever.

(The Evidence of Things Not Seen)

But it was Jimmy's life that puts such demonic tragedy in ever tightening jeopardy worldwide. He would not be still, he would not and never could be made to be just a mouthpiece for the prettily obscene. He sang of our lives and our needs and our will to triumph, even until his final hour.

Jimmy always made us feel good. He always made us know we were dangerously intelligent and as courageous as the will to be free!

Let us hold him in our hearts and minds. Let us make him part of our invincible black souls, the intelligence of our transcendence. Let our black hearts grow big world absorbing eyes like his, never closed. Let us one day be able to celebrate him like he must be celebrated if we are ever to be truly self-determining. For Jimmy was God's black revolutionary mouth. If there is a God, and revolution his righteous natural expression. And elegant song the deepest and most fundamental commonplace of being alive.

If we cannot understand our love of Jimmy Baldwin it is too late to speak of freedom or liberation, it has already been lost!

But it is his life that was confirmation of our love, and our love that is continuing proof that Hey, did you see Jimmy last night . . . you hear what he told so and so . . . part of our long slave narrative, as we speak to ourselves from within ourselves, and it is Jimmy's voice we hear, it has always been!

1987

Willie Jones (1929–1987)

Willie Jones

Willie
of all joneses
was an actual Jones
plus he was also
an actual Willie

together

No, it's all too real too funky
    too historical
    living image of our soul
    Both Willie & Jones

    The future & our entire
    identity
    real history

        makes our coat tails jump
        our toes tap tales our heels
        exaggerate

Us is a drum Us was the 1st Drum

        & can't be no drum
        unless we here
        & when we leave
        everything else will
            follow.

But dig, because
    we is both Willie

& Jones
The Future
& The Past

What was Willie is
also Jones
& what is Jones
was Willie
1st.

What hip Willie carried
we gave him
so he spread it
where he went
which gave more hip
to us & everybody else

I loved to see Willie, he made me remember
how BeBop saved me, & lifted me above the grey
tragedy of this regulation square death Shit.

He was a carrier, a messenger, of the spirit of the
Lord. Nut! Come is the Life The Light The Music
The Word!

Like a historical character in Pan African culture.
Willie, to see him was to be put in touch with the Music. And
that acknowledgment. The heavy
smack of our history. The renewed revelation of
Digging! Which the Squares will never dig.
& whose Stooges think it is technology
& murder explained into a menu

But, there on those twisting sidewalks,
inside those
all together out to lunch & back
"nightclubs"
& bars

```
& all the joints
   all them outside
downstairs
   anyplace
      joints

Where we might be in Hip
   and be hip
   & understand

We could exchange
   like treasure
   on any street
   of actual Hell
Great Joy  Great Vision  Great Love.
```

I always knew Willie Jones. In Newark, they graced those ghettoes like anonymous Princes, Block Boy Intellectuals, acknowledged artists. Philosophers who painted our neighborhoods with beauties of Word and example. Great thinkers who always remained deep in the soul of our actual oppressed lives.

The Willie Joneses of our selves is the source Cabral talked about in *Return to The Source*. In the culture is the historical and ultimate resistance to imperialism. And that is why the people, who are the repository of culture, in their lives and expression, create the constant geniuses that tell us always, somehow, who we are. Where we been. And in that, how to act.

Like the **Djali** (Griots) (Dig that? "Jelly, Jelly, Jelly"!) Willie carried the music, which is our history, the voice of our 2,500,000 years on the planet. He was a **Djali**. One of the "Fellahs," the desert brother, who amused themselves by singing history everywhere they went.

Ah, can you think of something hipper than meeting Willie on the street somewhere, where you could stand and run it for a minute?

The **value**, the critical **importance**, The actual **social** healing and **advance** of "The Music" would come out! How our Black

lives should be in all ways as Hip as The Music. as True as mean-
ingful as peaceful, as just

> as Godly

> as Holy

> as Swingin'

Because Willie Knew that Beauty & Truth
actually existed.

Marvin ("Pancho") Camillo (1937-1988)

Marvin Camillo

When I came back to live in Newark, in December 1965, after the prodigality of New York, and enforced military confinement, very shortly after I had begun to reconnect with this place, I came into contact with Marvin. Wilbur McNeil and Eugene Campbell asked me to direct my play, *Dutchman,* at Arts High, for their Calabar Arts Production Company. Marvin played Clay, the doomed, though heroically inspired youthful black intellectual confronted with death in the person of a crazed white female bohemian. Confronted with death by that image's essence, which is America, its promise, its malevolent seduction, and its characteristic destruction and murder.

Marvin was a shy person of enormous willingness and capacity. The essence of his skill was *desire*. He became what was intended, as the fruition of his own desire.

He was a penetrating observer, he watched, he listened closely. His Clay was rebellious, casually intelligent, full of the integrity of someone, at all costs, determined to be himself. Finally, true to his own feelings. What made his portrayal so telling and moving is that he is murdered by America even while openly despising it! The next year we worked together again in two of my plays, *Black Mass* and *JELLO*. Later, I directed him again in something called *Home on the Range*.

Marvin's sensitivity was his introduction to anyone. He carried it as his ultimate residence. It was the source of his art's power and communication. When he smiled, he made everyone happy because upon 1st encountering him we did not know whether it was possible or not. Though he smiled often!

But Marvin was part of the younger wave of Black Artists world wide, awakened and stimulated by the Civil Rights and Black Liberation movements of the '50s and '60s. He, like many of us, came to see our art as an important part of the total onslaught Black, Latino and oppressed people, worldwide, were making on white supremacy and social and economic exploitation. The transcendental revelations of art were directed toward the raising of human consciousness and the transformation of society. It was a commitment as deeply felt as any religion and perhaps ultimately more lasting!

Black Mass was my dramatization of Elijah Muhamad's story of Jacoub, the crazed black scientist who creates colorless monsters who resemble human beings. Their one flaw is they have no souls, no feeling, no sympathy for human life. Marvin was Tanzil, himself a highly developed scientist, who could not understand why the mad Jacoub would want to create such a monster. The very inhumanity of such a conception baffled him. Marvin made Tanzil wise yet still awed, in a sense, as to the extreme evilness of evil.

In *JELLO*, Marvin was Dennis Day, Jack Benny's Irish tenor. As Rochester (the late Yusef Iman) turned militant and proceeded to revile then rob Benny. Marvin leaped around the stage, caught in flight, yet frozen between belief and disbelief, terror and personal curiosity, even reverse admiration.

I mention these observations because they are among my deepest insights into this artist. And the most moving artists are fueled to their achievements by the direct workings of their feelings— their art a special mix of intellect and emotion.

Thinking about the world, its evil and ugliness, its logically explained frustration, probably could have made Marvin weep every hour of every day, like most of us who are not unconscious to one degree or another. But acting was *joy* to Marvin, his skillful biting characterizations, the undamning and justifications of his soul. He could soar as he spoke the lines, you felt the energy of his ecstasy, the brilliant fires detonated in his mind.

The fact that such transcendent happiness was blocked by this society was a large part of its terror for Marvin. Being Black in this land of celebrated white supremacy is oppressive, whatever your vocation. Being Black and wanting to commit your life to the creation of beauty and truth usually means you will be unemployed for great stretches. Or doing something else in order to eat.

It means you sometimes have to move around. Especially if born in the Newarks of this land, where employment as an artist comes only thru official bourgeois art and mostly employs official bourgeois (mostly white) artists and poseurs.

Marvin should have been director of a city-sponsored All City Drama Company, utilizing the talents of our own youth. His own sisters and brothers. And eventually (and in very recent history) and after much struggle, his world famous theater company *The Family* was given modest grants to stage a few productions.

But he had to go off into Vinnette Carroll's theater groups, then Urban Arts Corp. in NYC. He had to make his sojourn through Off Broadway, and Off Off Broadway to find a way back home.

Marvin founded *The Family* while working as a consultant for the Westchester NY Council for the Arts. It was this agency that got him into the Bedford Hills Correction Facility. It was his students from the prison and the high schools and colleges, in which he performed, from which *The Family* was formed. (Why not Newark's?)

He won awards as Best Director in 1973 and 1974. And in 1976, he directed Miguel Pinero's *Short Eyes* which won an OBIE for the Best Off Broadway Play. His discovery of Pinero brought *Short Eyes* to the Hollywood screen and made Pinero an internationally famous poet-dramatist (and actor-writer on *Miami Vice*), a celebrity.

Marvin built three different *Family* companies. One in NYC, one in Newark, and one in La Rochelle, France. Ironically, he went to France to die. But tonight they are holding a memorial for him in NYC at The Public Theater. And this morning we weep together that he has been brought home now to be buried. Would that we had celebrated him more while he was alive. Would that we had built theaters where he could delight and inspire us and educate our children, here in Newark where he was born and learned to love and hate, where he grew to manhood.

But that is part of the weakness that dissipated Marvin. Part of the animal callousness of these municipal slave quarters. Part of the cold oppression that forbids satisfaction, truth or beauty.

The Family was meant to focus on and raise the consciousness of and animate the victims of these terrifying cities. Particularly their Black and Latino indigents struggling to transcend the deadly limitations this society has put upon them. Marvin's company was a model of what these cities should build, Arts projects to strengthen and valorize inner city education.

Marvin was both Black and Latino, like much of the so-called Western World. It is a twain of geography and history, of culture and social life. *La Familia* was what Marvin meant in El Barrio. They called him "Pancho." Stretcher-bearer of happiness. He, himself, would tell you a little frankly.

His portrayal of a "Dad" of one of the average American families in *Home On The Range* convinced me he knew madness! He could imagine himself to be the thing he hated! But his life and concerns, the richness and fruitfulness of his labors, demonstrates the ultimate goodness and beauty of his pursuits. Their importance to all of us and the whole world!

Marvin used his life to create the things he loved and we all loved too and even desperately needed! When there is a popular public theater built in this city it should bear Marvin Camillo's name. It is the least we can do!!

If we were inspired by his intelligence, commitment, and creativity, we would bring his great ideas into being. We would create institutions to educate and raise our youth and employ and utilize our artists to transform our communities. In their institutions, in public institutions, in schools, and theaters and performance space in this city. We would inspire and employ them to speed our total development. To the extent to which their vision and intellect could be used to raise the very quality of all our lives here, together!

We are a people, Black, Latino, under constant attack and danger. We are subjects of street attacks, subway massacres, conspiracies, attempted genocide, national oppression. John Killens, Harold Washington and James Baldwin have died in the last month. Whoever loved these brothers must pick up their gauntlet, accept the swift baton. We must celebrate our fallen by word and by deed!

Evidence of Marvin's love for the world is everywhere, let us show our love for Marvin in the same fashion±openly and dramatically, as part of that popular force which must one day shape this world so that it will finally show its love for Marvin! By saying goodbye to the animal world.

Rest In Change
Noble Brother
Your life is
part of our
Being!

1988

Kasisi Sadikifu Nakawa
Paul Arnold Sanders (1945-1988)

Nakawa

In the late '60s, after the massive Newark uprising, which signaled, as in the other major U.S. Cities with large black populations, that colonialism was on its death bed!, I met Paul Sanders Nakawa, along with dozens of other young people from around the county and state, ultimately from around the country.

They were drawn into Newark by the vehemence and enraged fighting spirit of the people. These were young African Americans, emboldened by the great leader Malcolm X, not only to resist white supremacy and the national oppression of our people, but also to seek out their own historic and cultural origins, as the flag and war cry of the newest wave of the Black Liberation Movement!

Nakawa, his name means "Good Looking & Healthy," as all of us were, young, beautiful, strong and arrogant. We felt we were the generation, the culmination of Black Struggle around the world, finally to deliver black people from our international oppressors and laughingly, while slapping our palms and signifying, take the beast's head for once and for all! It was not if, but **when!** And we meant to speed the when up to **in a minute, right around the corner!** No, we were **bad!!**

Nakawa and some of the brothers and sisters I'm looking at right now moved back and forth between the west coast cultural nationalist movement *US* and what finally came to be called CFUN and CAP in Newark.

And when Newark did become the center of the Black Liberation Movement, after the Black Power Conference of 1967 held just after the 1967 rebellion, and then with the electoral victory of Kenneth Gibson, as Mayor and three other black councilmen in 1970, Nakawa joined our Newark centered CAP and took up a leadership position, as we put together the historic Atlanta *Con-*

gress of African Peoples Conference in 1970 to gain **Black Power!**

He was our advanced political cadre we sent to Gary, Indiana to make final logistical arrangements for the 1972 National Black Political Convention, where some 8,000 Black people met to organize a permanent National Black Political Assembly across the U.S. to take up the struggle for Black Power, i.e., Self-Determination and Democracy!

The Rainbow Coalition, which Jesse Jackson used to carry him to Atlanta, was, in fact, an extension of the Gibson campaign (with its Rainbow logo) and the Gary convention. Jackson, himself, came out of both those gatherings, but unlike Atlanta '88, we talked and organized to struggle for **Black Power!**

Nakawa was not just a dedicated activist in that great struggle, indeed, he was one of our brightest young leaders. Make no mistake he, like all of the best of us then, was **serious!** We were Black Revolutionaries in love with Revolution!

But there have been several oceans of water under the proverbial bridge since then! There has been, as always and forever, constant change, many times, barely understood!

Since then, we have seen many black militants regress to unmilitant silly negroes! We have seen not a few of our leaders elected to office off the backs of the black masses turn into spitoons of reaction!

Many of us, including Paul, moved on past cultural nationalism, to internationalism. He, as a member of the Revolutionary Workers' League and the "Revolutionary Wing" and other more recent Marxist-Leninist organizations. We have struggled to correctly understand our time, place and conditions here in the U.S. and have grown in our collective struggle to reach a correct analysis of not only white supremacy and racism, but also to understand that these outrages are the products of Imperialism. An international system which has enslaved the masses of the world to a handful of monopoly capitalist nations.

Paul Nakawa gave his adult life and half his youth to righteous struggle against our enemies. This is one of the tragic assaults his death must confront us with, because no matter whether our analysis and commitment to struggle to change this animal-ruled hell was identical with Paul's or not, we must celebrate this brother, this militant, this comrade, not only because he was steeled in real struggle, but because we knew his sincerity and commitment was for life!

And we have lost another seasoned leader. Another patriotic African revolutionary whose leadership we need and whose replacement will be difficult! We have already lost too many! Because many of us think of our activism as a product of the romantic '60s! We pine for the old Civil Rights movement, when the real civil rights movement is **now**, still!!

And worse, this society is careening, especially since the inception of the Reagan years, toward **Fascism**. And too many of us live in the past or else we are held captive in the present by opportunism, or like most, lack of revolutionary organization.

Nakawa was a brother of great courage and dynamism. He moved from phase to phase in his development like many of us, searching for the correct form, the advanced organization, the mass line, to propel us all, again, into revolutionary movement!

The problems that face us today are still dangerous and draining. We face the summation and necessary tactical movement to counter the Second Atlanta Compromise, this summer at the Democratic convention.

Also, the cooptation of a growing sector of the Black National Bourgeoisie and Petty Bourgeoisie into proto comprador elements, using the smoke screen of anti-drug rhetoric, to set up more and more intense anti-black-working-class, neo-fascist structures in our community.

Here in Newark, we are witness to a microcosm of the same abomination, with some black elected officials openly and publicly lobbying to curtail our democratic rights, for instance, around the question of our elected school board (for which Nakawa fought so hard) rather than expand our democracy!

There is still neither bowling alley nor movie theater in Newark and Symphony Hall has been given away to the corporations, along with an increasing amount of our own tax money.

At yesterday's State Championship Basketball game, in which one Newark school, University High participated, there was not one elected official, nor representative of the Board of Education,

City Hall or the City Council, yet these same paid bureaucrats continue to blame our children for their own shortcomings. The student take-over of a building at Howard University* shows how dramatically opposed to these opportunistic Negro bureaucrats our youth can be. And Nakawa was a model and organizer of youth all his political life. (I know Nakawa you would love and be proud of our son, Ras.)

A life finally dedicated to the smashing of the bourgeois state and the building of a socialist state and ultimately classless communism.

The Afro-American people are still an oppressed nation engaged in a National Liberation struggle, at the same time we are part of the struggle of the American working people of all nationalities to smash U.S. monopoly capitalism and imperialism forever.

I mention these things because Paul Sanders/Nakawa was passionately committed to these goals. And I know his spirit would be unfulfilled unless this call was sounded over his earthly remains! Because he was, since I knew him, a revolutionary. This was our bond, this was our life!

So now at the crossroads of another valued militant's leaving, prematurely, Mhisani, Jomo, Sonni Koontz, Nsongi, Sandi Smith and in the wake of the Second Great Atlanta compromise, let us all now recommit ourselves, rededicate ourselves and let us not forget, **reorganize** ourselves, for the purpose our people and the greatest of our leaders have struggled for and cried and shouted and sung and whispered and died for since we were brought here in the bottom of the slave ships: SELF-DETERMINATION and with that, the liberation of all humanity. Let us recommit our selves in Paul Sanders', Nakawa's name and with the most glorious examples of his revolutionary's life

    Just Pushin The Program,
    Comrade
    Just Pushin The Program

---

*Led by Ras Baraka, and a student group.

Miguel Piñero (1946-1988)

Hail Mikey!

I

Poets Miguel Algarin and Nancy Mercado mentioned to another poet, my wife Amina, that writer Miguel "Mikey" Piñero was having a birthday, and he was in the hospital, recuperating from America.

Amina thought we needed to pull together a celebration of artists and friends to let Miguel know a lot of people love him and his work and wish him a long, productive life.

Piñero's great friend, Miguel Algarin, was next enlisted as well as myself. And the word went out. We called New Jersey and New York literary connections, good friends, and the generally enlightened. We got poets and musicians and painters and dancers and filmmakers and good partiers.

Interestingly, at the same moment (guided by Amina) that this set was being put together, the International PEN Organization was having its congress with writers and intellectuals from all over the world. There had even been a few political outbreaks with some writers objecting to Reagan's Secretary of State, Schultz, giving the opening address and stating it openly at the session. Norman Mailer seemed, from the vantage point of some congress-absent readers, to be more upset by what he termed writers' "silly impoliteness" than the fact of the world-advertised backwardness of his keynote speaker.

Later, Betty Friedan would lead a demonstration charging that there were not enough women in decision-making positions. Norman sounded equally as weird, toe-dancing around this obvious truism. Though, to be sure, I'm sure there were even fewer Blacks (men or women) and Latinos than "women." On the positive side, the conference did create a context in which a variety of significant international figures could contribute to Mikey's tribute.

Piñero, the author of the acclaimed stage drama and film *Short*

Eyes, won the New York Drama Critics Award and the OBIE (off Broadway) citation (in 1974) for this work, a brutal look at prison degeneration and repression.

Piñero has also written important, penetrating poetry of an open anti-establishment cast, hot, raging, and as funny as his portrait of "God" in *The Gospel According to St. Miguelito* as a junky with a snotty nose with "his Jones coming down on him."

He was co-editor with Miguel Algarin of *NuYorican Poetry* a signal anthology (published by William Morrow) of new, mostly New York based Puerto Rican poets. Pedro Pietri (*Puerto Rican Obituary*); Jose Angel Figueroa (*Across 116th Street*) were some of the most impressive writers to emerge from that group.

Algarin opened the NuYorican Poets Cafe on East Second Street of "Loisaida" (the Lower East Side, the funkier end of "The East Village"). It was a crossroad of Puerto Rican, other Latino, Black and third world poets and other writers who had a taste for what's happening now.

My own *What Was the Relationship of the Lone Ranger to the Means of Production* opened there with Taylor Mead, Judith Kallas, Ngoma & Jaribu Hill of *Serious Bizness* and Yusef Iman.

What made the party so rich was not only did a bunch of old friends and new acquaintances get together, but we did so to show the strength of our affection for Mikey himself and his work and all works we know to be in essence commonly focused at some point on human liberation.

The day of the set other old friends came to help Amina get the show up on time. Furaha Rosita Broadus, an actress with the old Spirit House, Beth Minsky a paralegal worker, helped get the basics together. Later, culinary anthropologist Verta Mae Grosvenor arrived to pitch in.

At Amina's suggestion, I had called Newark City Councilman (now Mayor since 1986) Sharpe James to get the City Council to present Miguel with a proclamation from the City. I'd also asked the Theater of Universal Images' Clarence Lilly, also head of the local cable company (Connection Cable Co.), to cover the goings on and he did.

Our new superintendent of schools, Eugene Campbell (ironically the first Newark-born superintendent of schools since Black Mayor Ken Gibson's 1970 election!) was in evidence. But an added highlight with very important political overtones was the appearance at the party of Omar Cabeza, the Nicaraguan novelist, and his wife, and exiled Guatemalan film maker, Arturo Arias (*El Norte*) who gave an international tone to the set that was as relevant as it was joyous.

I introduced Miguel Algarin who introduced Mikey and then Councilman James read the proclamation. Amina had our children and their friends greet Mikey in a formal and gratifying display of community and family self-respect.

Then Arias greeted the guests but it was Commandante Cabeza who transformed the partygoers into a cheering group of "anti-interventionists" when he charged this country with preparing to invade Nicaragua and turn the country back to an American-owned slave state.

Amina summed up the gathering and related world struggles to our own in the U.S. and potentially to the revolution raging in South Africa and U.S. backward racist support of the Apartheid white supremacy government in South Africa.

But we partied and the talk in Spanish and American lifted in laughter and toasts and dancing. Plus at a party full of artists, especially poets, there's got to be some reading, plus the normal dancing and singing.

Puerto Rican cuisine, African American cuisine and Jewish cuisine were all in evidence. Tito Puente, B. B. King, Bob Marley, Potato & Totico, Billie Holiday, and John Coltrane all got played. New York City 1950's "Palladium" steps, Reggae "Jump Up," Jitterbug and the Moonwalk got displayed.

Furaha recited Amina's poem *Nicaragua On My Mind*, one striking line, "Hands off Nicaragua, you who protect the Klan and Nazis." She also recited Dr. King's "I Have A Dream" speech and a visible thrill went through a crowd suddenly put in touch with the spirit of the '60s Civil Rights struggle, part of the international struggle for democracy and self-determination still going on around the world.

II

Obviously the above was written just before Mikey booked. This is what Amina felt then, that he was gonna be outta here soon. Miguel Algarin had also voiced this, sad to say, we all did, even Mikey.

But today, in this place, knowing Mikey has cut out and Miguel has wandered through the Loisaida spreading his ashes, it still brings you low. I see my old friend, Joe Papp, the producer, over there, alive and well, (how come producers always seem to be alive and well, years after the people who made them rich and famous have split?—no offense, Joe!) and wonder how is it Mikey, little screwed up brilliant Mikey, so much younger and stronger, and along with so many others like him, already gone. And God, to think about it, to name them, just a few bright stars around the NuYorican Poets' Cafe . . . Loparaina, Cienfuegos, Papaleto, Dr. Willie, so quickly, so much fire so much promise, and yet the madman world lay breathing ugly in wait for them to cut them down. Like Larry Neal, (another bright light put out) said, Tell them, "I was a bad mf, but the butcher cut me down."

It means we will be nothing but batteries for somebody else's flashlight until we get our own. And ain't that what the NuYorican and our own *Kimako's* in Newark are trying to agitate!

Mikey Piñero was a great poet, an important playwright, and a working actor. His screenplay, *Short Eyes* (which received the 1974 Obie Award for the Best American Play, and the American Book Award), was made into an exciting commercial film, with Mikey playing one of the leads. Trying to describe him to the many nonliterary humans, I kept saying, "You know, he played the drug king pin, Calderon, in *Miami Vice*." His wd be Hollywood bailout which was actually a bail in.

If Mikey was ever trying to get away from the wheel of Hell which characterized much of his personal life, Holly Wood, and did not, help. In a way, it only glamorized his descent into constant trauma.

But check the poetry in the anthology he helped edit with Algarin, *NuYorican Poetry*, which is one of the most important

books of contemporary Latino verse. My all time Mikey favorite is *The Book of Genesis According To Saint Miguelito*. I love to read it aloud. As a matter of fact I even read it for Mikey and the whole crew at that last party we gave. Just check a little bit:

> On the fourth day
> God was riding around Harlem in a gypsy cab
> when he created the people
> and he created these beings in ethnic proportion
> but he saw the people lonely & hungry
> and from his eminent rectum
> he created a companion for these people
> and he called this companion
> capitalism
> who begat racism
> who begat exploitation
> who began male chauvinism
> who begat machismo
> who begat imperialism
> who begat colonialism
> who begat wall street
> who begat foreign wars
> and God knew
> and God saw
> and God felt this was extra good
> and God said
> "VAYAAAAAAAA"

That was Mikey. I remember the 1st day I met him and Miguel Algarin out in Colorado frightening the white folks. A long way from the Loisaida, where Mikey had emerged as the ultimate street person, a characterization that drove him way past reason.

But in my sadness, the desperate frustration of facing the early deaths of my brilliant brothers and sisters all over the planet, listen to this self opening look at Mikey by himself:

he died yesterday
he's dyin' today
he's dead tomorrow
died seekin' a Cause
died seekin' the Cause
& the Cause was in front of him
& the Cause was in his skin
& the Cause was in his speech
& the Cause was in his blood
but
he died seekin' the Cause
he died seekin' a Cause
he died
deaf
dumb
&
blind
he died
died
& never found his Cause
because
you see he never never
knew that he was the
Cause

Mikey Piñero, mi hermano sangre, dead at 41.

1988

Joseph S. ("Smiley") Landrum (1935-1989)

"My Joe" Funeral Oration

Joseph "Smiley" Landrum was one of those solid rock working people of which our Newark community and indeed the American and African American nation are fundamentally composed. They are the basic creators, the production movers and shakers upon which all nations depend for their sustenance and development.

In the U. S., a great deal is made of the "rich & famous." There are tv shows, countless films, unending magazine and newspaper accounts of the folks with the big bux or high finance lifestyles or media-created superstars. We are trained publicly to worship, to envy, to be controlled by, the wealthy. To aspire to their lives, and take on, to the extent this is possible, their world view.

So more of us know more about Donald Trump than James Baldwin. We are more intimate with Malcolm Forbes's obscene billion dollar parties than the need most of us have to build a third party. Rockefeller is immortalized in popular songs, even tho a murderer.

But the basic, the most common fabric of our society are the working people, and they are still largely anonymous and unsung. Joe Landrum was such a man and while this brief moment is also something of a song for him, so that even in this form he will no longer be totally unsung, still there is something deeper you should know. About Joe, why finally he was important, not just to our long time sister-in-arms, Tina Johnson, Takalifu, but to us all.

You see part of Joe's song was Takalifu, that's Sister Tina Johnson's swahili name for any Johnny-come-latelies in the house. Takalifu, and the entire family is also part of Joe's song. You see, for working people, the real creators of society, of both people and objects and relationships, they are sung, realized, by those creations. Though we should know, in this exploitive and oppressive society, that the working class majority cannot even create

what is needed by the majority to advance society because the Forbeses and the Trumps and the Rockefellers &c own the tools, the land, the mineral wealth, the communications, 6/10ths of one percent owning all the tools and the other 99&1/2% of the people as well—including city hall, the housing authority and the board of education.

Takalifu was the swingingest part of Joe's song. And even though some of us did not know Joe well, the laughing jovial brother, always spreading that little light of his around so all of us could get a little, chances are if we were educated to the politics of Newark education, we knew or know of Tina/Takalifu, that little laughing ball of dynamism and community activism.

Tina has headed up the *Peoples' Democratic Council Committee to Save The Children*, for several years, and even ran for the Newark Board of Education. She is always in the thick of the good fight, both seen and heard. What is so important for us to understand is that her husband and lover for 26 years, Joseph Landrum, backed all of her activities to the max.

Joe Landrum, like many working people, had two jobs. Maybe that's what helped kill him so young, at 53. A life of hard work and maximum stress. He worked for the post office as a mail handler, he also worked for the Newark Board of Education as a bus attendant for handicapped children. And Joe was a father, a grandfather, and recently even a great grandfather.

Born in that part of the city we used to call "Down Neck," on Bruen St., Joe Landrum made many many friends in the post office and board of education over the years and throughout the city. He was a good union man as well, and served as a group leader and spent many hours on the phone and in meetings counciliating workers' disputes. In other words, Joe was a class-conscious worker, one of the advanced, whose efforts make the whole movement go forward.

Joe and Tina's is a real love story. And even though he could not be present at the interminable round of meetings and rallies and marches that Tina/Takalifu was always at the head of, he was the bedrock, the solid foundation upon which any lasting structure must be built.

Tina could be at all these manifestations of progressive African American political motion because Joe provided the means, the backup, not just economic, but the spritiual support, the human encouragement, that bonding of will to will that makes a larger more forceful will. What keeps so many of us who are out front going. Without that solid backup, that spiritual nourishing back home, we could do nothing but stutter and stumble, and instead of being heroes, we would be very very humble.

One thing the detractors of working people and detractors of African American people, specifically those who are always putting down black and latino men for not being present at different political struggles, while the women are. There is some truth to this accusation, but we should also keep in mind Joe Landrum, bcause there are a bunch of Joe Landrums or José Landrums, who are the homefront, solid as a rock, backups. Whose wives or female companions might be out front battling but who support their wives' work, who support our community's development. The Joes who make the Tinas possible. It used to be we would say behind every great man there is a woman; now we can say, as well, behind every great woman there is a great man.

Joe even enabled Tina to go back to school at the middle age of her life, and get her degree. Joseph Landrum was no male chauvinist; he had got beyond Macho Man to Revolutionary Man.

So we must now sing Joseph Landrum. He cannot be unsung any longer. When we see Tina or any of the children—moving through or doing progressive work in the community, remember it is part of Joe's song. Now all of us need to help sing that song, ever louder and ever stronger. Along with Tina/Takalifu.

We need to help Tina strengthen the *People's Democratic Council Committe To Save The Children*. Because our children are in trouble. Attacked and put down by the very people the society pays to protect and nurture them. The next time you hear some foolish political pimp castigating our children for the city or nation's messed up existence, tell them, Hey, the children dont get paid to run the city or nation! And that will be part of Joe's song.

When you hear them jumping on our children as if it was the young black boys with their hats turned around backwards bopping into these county jails tricked by imperialism. When you call out to decriminalize drugs and take the profit motive out and stop killing our children. Hey, you will be singing part of Joe's song.

When they want to use the fake war on drugs to wage a real war on our children and get ready for another war in Latin America under the guise of drug interdiction, another bloodier Vienam. Say, Hey, Bush, I can read through that, and you will be singing Joe's song.

If you start telling folks how we need a civilian police review board, Sister Tina/Takalifu is on that case already, we need board so we can conduct testing of these beasts in blue to see if they have been damaged unalterably by racism. You will be singing, like the rest of us, Joe's song.

And if you start saying we need psychological testing for racism on all public employees, including teachers, and that we need black studies, Latino studies, Spanish as a second language, and artists in residence in the schools, then you will be singing, no, you will be really wailing Joe's song and then see Joe will be there with us, in spirit, that spirit, animating us, filling us, still holding little live Takalifu's hand, and then you will, like all the rest of us, be singing Joe's song. And it will be smoking. It will be smee-zok-ing!!!! Tutaonana Joe!

1989

John Alexander (1919-1990)

Dr. John W. Alexander, M.D.

At Dr. Alexander's funeral, I was asked to read the famous poem of Sterling Brown's (my English teacher at Howard University), "Strong Men."

But I wanted also to register these things, as a kind of eulogy not given at the funeral, that is more of detailed intimacy than the poem, as great as it is.

Dr. Alexander and I met when he, literally, saved my second son Ras's life in 1969. One day, Amina had become aware that Ras' seemed very sleepy and drowsy. He was then less than one year old. She tried everything to rouse him and it seemed he only got drowsier. She went to one doctor who told her the child was lethargic. We knew that. She called others and finally someone referred her to Dr. Alexander.

When we went to see him, he got to the root of the problem right away. In some way, Ras, who was always crawling across the Spirit House floors, had got ahold of some phenobarbitol, from somewhere—we didn't even smoke cigarettes. And it was this drug that was not only making him drowsy but threatening, ultimately, to take his young life.

We were in a state near hysteria when Dr. Alexander made his diagnosis. He quickly shaved the sides of young Ras's head and cut into his ankles, draining the poisonous drug away.

That night he even allowed Amina to sleep in the hospital room with the boy, which was probably a first. In the years that followed, Amina and the woman's division of our organization, CFUN/CAP worked with Dr. Alexander very closely around health matters concerning the organization and the community at large.

For instance, under Dr. Alexander's leadership, the community was given much more access to both the city hospital and Presbyterian, particularly around maternity cases. This had been more common in the suburbs than the inner city larger Black and Latino patiented hospitals.

Amina was even a member of a community board to relate community needs and programs to the overall policy of the city hospital. All this, of course, during the political upsurge of the '60s and '70s.

But in a real way, Dr. Alexander was part of that Black political upsurge. He was our lightning rod at the hospital, a brilliant and caring physician who was also good at fighting for the people!

I remember in 1972 Amina and I took all our then born kids (Amiri Jr. was riding in the hangar and Ahi wasn't even thought of yet, Shani was a teeny tot) to Trinidad, including the four girls by Amina's and my own 1st marriages. That was seven kids (Obalaji, Ras, Shani, Vera, Wanda, Kellie and Lisa)!

A very wild trip that. When we got there, as Mr. & Mrs. Everett Jones, a guy jumped out of the side lines and embraced me saying, "Imamu, Imamu!"

A customs official(?) then charged out and ultimately emptied our luggage of all revolutionary literature. Later, a man sat by the pool with us, with his street clothes on, the entire week of our trip.

And then to top it off, little Shani comes down with a case of outrageous diarrhea. We were at our wits' end, until we remembered to call home. Call Dr. Alexander. And sure enough, he gave us the address of a doctor right there in Port of Spain where his baby-curing counterpart lived.

Whenever we called upon Dr. Alexander, through the years he responded, in his engaging, intelligent fashion. One time we even got into a group of people that included Dr. Alexander, trying to purchase radio station WNJR as a base for community development.

Dr. Alexander was of that seemingly steadily diminishing species, the Black professional sincerely interested in the people's development. Rare anytime, Dr. Alexander was one of the diverse forces called to the front by the foaming '60s. A highly skilled professional who was still on the side of the working class. Part of that revolutionary class alliance, led by working people, that will eventually topple this sad oppressive society.

All our children sat under Dr. Alexander's stethoscope at one time or another. And they will always have memories of this good strong man. One of those who, as Sterling Brown said, keep on coming.

1990

Walter Davis, Jr. (1932-1990)

Walter Davis, Jr.

I know there's all kinds of people here. Family, Relatives, Old Friends, Diggers of The Music, Musicians and Artists and just different people who knew Walter. It's weird, there's no politicians here, the city fathers and what not. Walter was known around the world as a great musician, one of the stomp down original funkateers, straight out of Buhainia's hippest bag.

But it just shows you where we issssss. And who's running stuff. But whoever's here, however, you know this brother. This marvelous pianist of the Newark slick hip bebop and blues based rhythm piano. The many fingered flat fives and oopapadows. The soul rising way-out and all the way-in stuff.

You know, like Walter, when you saw him. We used to call him "Humphrey," with his red freckle face smiling yellow buddha in a well-cut vine self.

Whenever I saw Walter the whole place lit up, like that smile. That universal, "you dig it?" smile—that was lights. And Walter played music, teeth and mouth hipster rhythm scatting his breath when he met you. "Hey Me-an . . . What's Happening?"

Like he was carrying the sun and it made him bubble. When it came back from where it went, going through him. "Hey Me-an." And you would bubble with him. The all time downster of my age. From early. "Hey, Me-an," you know like a drawl, a spread out chord arpeggio that brought him in cool yet that boppish timbre like a riff.

My man. He would light up everything. You know, like everything would get at least funny. It could be the street the sidewalk the gig he had, Monk's weirdness, traveling with Buhainia, a benefit, the latest side, who was at the Five Spot, what Jackie McLean said last night.

You know, because, 1st, meeting Walter would make you happy.

And you felt hip talking to Walter. With his weird looking, Asian looking Blood self, them squinched up laughing eyes and puffy cheeks. "What's happnin Me-an?" I mean the hip shit.

Walter Davis Jr. was one of the legends of my growing up. Like Wayne Shorter and Woody Shaw and Grachan Moncur III and Sarah Vaughan and Moody and Hank Mobley at the Howard Bar, and Len and Len's and The Key Club. He played with Bird, Diz, was one of Art Blakey's funkiest Messengers.

Walter played with some of the most important and best known artists in the world, the masters. Sonny Rollins, Betty Carter, plus he was always inside where the hip was going. Check him out with avant master, Archie Shepp on Attica Blues or Way Ahead. He consistently had his own groups, trios, duos, quartets and recorded as a leader. Remember, Davis Cup?

Actually, Walter was one of the coolest dudes I knew. He looked like BeBop. It came out of his face and eyes and mouth and definitely out of his fingers. He was slightly round, just enough to look like he knew what he was doing. But in that musical stylish way, like the nice threads he always showed up in, just enough to make people call him Humphrey, hip and funny with just enough irony to Bogart squares or sit on them with the music.

If there ever was a Bopper, on the serious side, it was Hip Humphrey from Newark, Walter Davis, Jr. And dig this, no matter how cold and corny it is or gets in this place ruled by United Squares, or how somber and quiet and drugged we get and make this funeral, I know that wherever he is, Walter is swinging even harder than when you heard him. Wherever he is, something very hip is happening!

Hey, Me-aaann . . .

1990

James ("Omar") Gray (1963-1990)

Remember Omar

Once again we come together to mourn one of our fallen children. Today, another man-child slaughtered by imperialism. Again, a wanton bleeding of all of us, through our babies. These same babies we swore to transform the world to save!

Young Omar, James Gray, just 27 years old. Son of Donald and Rosa Lee Gray. Cut down in these grim chaotic streets, murdered for the same reasons as the others. Being Black and alive and the child of working people!*

James, who took the name Omar, one of the prophet Muhammad's generals and advisers. Also the name of the great poet and mathematician.

He took the name, like all of us who took on African and Islamic names, to signify it was a new day (a new world). To signify that we would no longer be slaves, that we had moved to become, as the great Du Bois advised, truly **self-conscious**, meaning that we had transcended the psychological sickness caused by our slave and national oppression, the psychological disease created by our being taught to look at ourselves through the eyes of people that hate us.

But today, we ought to expand our grief so that it also includes **self-revelation**. So that our grief serves also to open our eyes and teach us who and where we are. So that our grief begins to educate us as to who are our friends and who are our enemies!

Why is young Omar, the righteous seed of righteous parents, here dead before us while we weep? Why is it Omar dead and not a Klansman or the butchers that murdered Eleanor Bumphurs, or the killers of Black youths at Bensonhurst and Howard Beach?

---

*James tried to intervene in a dispute as a peacemaker and was killed by someone he didn't know.

Why is Omar dead rather than the blue-suit racist fiends that every day beat and lock up our children or the monsters who raped Tawana Brawley or murdered Philip Panell in Teaneck?

Why? Omar? Lying here dead and we helpless and mourning.

Why is my oldest son Obalaji in prison, my son, Ahi recovering from being shot in the head this summer?

Why are the jails filled with us, our children, wall to wall? Is it that we are evil? Do we deserve so much pain and suffering? Are we created by God for poverty and endless frustration? As our enemies tell us everyday!

Let our grief move us through this pain to understanding. Let it clear our heads. Let our weeping wash our eyes and cleanse our hearts. Let our sorrow fill our hearts with black fire, so that their very beating will speak to us, touch us, move us to better understand, what must be done. What must be done to transform this bleeding jungle of a city, this wilderness ruled by vicious capitalist animals and killer white supremacists. Let our weeping and relentless pain teach us clearly what must be done, what we must do, we who are still alive. Not just our biological bodies, but those of us who can still feel! Those of us who have not sold, or given away or destroyed, our immortal (human) souls!!

Omar was born in 1963. Just seven years before we triumphed (we thought), we righteous oppressed Blacks and Puerto Ricans and our allies, just 7 years before we rose up with one mighty blow to smash these local fiends who oppressed us.*

They were **white**! we screamed. These devils who were in charge of our future. But we would no longer submit! We screamed Black Power! Unity without Uniformity! We had organized and worked 24 hrs a day. We argued and lectured and canvassed and put up posters and struggled and fought. Fought! We fought landlords and cops and corporate assassins and backward house niggers and racists and politicians! We made punks out of overweight fascist psychotics who threatened us on TV with tanks and automatic weapons and racist stupidity! But the constant

---

**In 1970, Kenneth Gibson was elected Mayor of Newark. He was the first African-American Mayor of a major urban center in the northeast.

description of our motion was that we **fought**. We fought. We resisted and signified and worked and gathered, in our righteous indignation, in caucuses, and endless meetings, and even conventions, and like modern revolutionaries, we planned and did not B.S. but **actually** produced and finally, yes, we won! Yes, we triumphed. We destroyed American Apartheid (**No**, it ain't just in South Africa, **Americans invented Apartheid!!!** On us!!!)

And prominent in that righteous peoples' movement for Afro-American Self-Determination and American People's Democracy were parents of James (Omar) Gray, Donald and Rosa Gray!

Rosa Gray was and is a legend in this town. Her name is synonymous, for those who been there, for those who know. When you say **Rosa Gray**, you talking about a Newark version of Fannie Lou Hamer. A contemporary Harriet Tubman.

Rosa Gray means activist in this town. A righteous Black peoples' activist struggling for that **higher ground**, that new day, that new world to transform this society now, where we live, to force democracy, and equality. **Rosa Gray** means an advanced fighter for what Malcolm called for Self-Determination, Self-Respect and Self-Defense.

That's why our enemies would quake in their socks when **Rosa Gray**'s name was called or when their secretaries would call over the intercom that there was a **Rosa Gray** in the outer office waiting to jump in their saggy behinds and pour verbal lighter fluid on the stolen clothes they covered their lies with.

This is Omar Gray's mother. And our righteous struggle was the context of Omar's infancy and early childhood!

But then, why is he dead like this? Why is he laying here now before us, soaking up our tears with lifelessness?!

Is this what Donald and Rosa fought for? Was this what we meant when we screamed **Black Power** and punched out racists in these streets?

No! No! No! No! It was **not** for **this**!

Donald and Rosa, like all of us who fought to replace the racists' choice, the bankers' choice, with The Community Choice.

We did not fight to see our youth shot down in the streets by paid or volunteer maniacs. Just as we did not fight to see them mashed flat in these prisons or dying violently from the profitable hypocrisy of the money launderers' refusal to decriminalize and regulate drugs and end the same kind of violence and exploitation and corporate profiteering that accompanied the prohibition of liquor! A great deal of the political and corporate power that the immigrant Irish, Italians and Jews obtained and expanded in this society came from bootlegging illegal alcohol!

We did not fight to see our children murder each other out of ignorance and frustration and their victimization by this slave society.

We did not fight to see them daily miseducated and taught to hate themselves and despise their parents.

Just as our rulers daily scream at us that it is our children who are the devils who created and govern and profit from this Hell!

Our slave masters teach us every day, at the top of their voices, that it is our children who are evil. Violent evil niggers and spics! They are souped up mindless muggers and defilers of this otherwise peaceful beautiful democratic paradise!!

Rosa Gray fought so that Omar could grow and be educated and find the work he wanted and raise a healthy family in a productive egalitarian society in which love was the common bond and language!

But **wait**. We **know** we fought. Rosa and Donald know. Omar knew as their other children must understand, that Rosa and Donald, like my wife Amina and I, **fought** and still fight for a world in which Omar and all our Omars and Tawanas and Yusefs and Obalajis could grow into beautiful Black men and women and begin the **self-rule** of the **people**!!

But **look** at the coffin again and let it tell you, cold as Omar's death, that we have been **betrayed**. Yes, **Betrayed**! That all of us, not just the fighters like Rosa and Donald or us Barakas and all of you I see out there, but **all of us** who would **live** in a righteous world of brothers and sisters, living our lives in emulation of Love, the creator.

But we are what we **actually** are, not what we might **think** we are! In our resistance to racism and white supremacy, we failed to understand the phenomenon of **Class**. We are all **Black** and **Racism** oppressed us all **equally**. But it is better to suffer racism in a penthouse than in Scudder Homes. It is better to be discriminated against as a college graduate than if you are a domestic worker, or truck driver, or work on an assembly line!

When we smashed the local political structure of American Apartheid in 1970, electing a Black mayor and councilmen, we were leaders of our people everywhere! City after city followed our lead. In South Africa today, they are still struggling to destroy this **Racial Nazism**.

But we raised too many collaborators and agents of slavery, who wore black skin as camouflage. We elected too **many middle-**class prostitutes and white-skin worshippers. For many of these middle class petty bourgeois negroes (yes, that's what Malcolm called them, **Negroes**, unreconstructed **House** Negroes) hate us **much worse** than they hate our enemies. They are **more frightened** of us than the Klan!!

They tell us our children are too criminalistic! We are too militant. Too Black! Too loud! Too ignorant! Too uncool!! To live as well as they do. We don't deserve to have good jobs or have clean newly painted houses. We are too niggerish to be employed. We **love** welfare! We **want** to live in slums! We don't **value** education, that's why we are uneducated! (I guess that's why little Minnie Jean Brown had to go to Little Rock High with a division of paratroopers!!!)

No, the truth is we have raised, **as our leaders**, a class of negroes with neither **courage** nor **intelligence**, with neither testicles nor smarts! This narrow class, who blocks the door of freedom with their backward betraying lives.

Omar was 7 in 1970! It is 20 years later. He should have been helping to **run** this city. He was one of our most energetic and hard working and popular youths. The cream of our lives! Yet he is struck down, because now these streets are more dangerous, the people more insane, than when we mobilized to take control of this city and our lives! 20 years ago!

But look, Rosa and Donald did **not** become powerful, well-heeled administrators or municipal Honchos. They, for all their work and struggle, have received, like most of us, **nothing** for our efforts but frustration and pain! **Nothing** but **betrayal!**

Those who took power on our backs have turned their backs on us and can discuss our tragedy casually, at tennis courts and on charming islands. So important, they can hang out with Powerful Devils!

They can speak to us hypnotically about "Renaissance in Newark" and not be talkin about where we live, not be speaking about us, the majority, they ain't even talkin about us. No, not at all!

Their children are not in jail or murdered senselessly. The police are not sweeping their children off street corners in their own neighborhoods, or beating their parents and brothers and sisters.

They are not unemployed! They work for us, they say. The Newark Education budget is almost 500 million a year. The city hall budget over 400 million. That means we ought to have **1 billion dollars a year** at our disposal to change our lives! Yet where is it? Who's got it?

Was any of it spent to prevent our son Omar's murder, a victim of slavery still?

But now, a slavery sanctioned and presided over by alienated important negroes, who are ashamed of us only slightly more than their ignorant no heart selves!

They learned it in school, that's why they won't change the curriculum, after they swore us to do it 20 years ago to all the people of Newark! Not just to the militants. They swore to change our schools, to get rid of the racist curriculum, 20 years ago.

They lied and drank cocktails and collaborated with those who have brought the city down in ruins and vacant lots around our ears. They made money and went on vacations and we still have no jobs, only poor housing, racist miseducation in crumbling schools. We are the AIDS Center. A Trauma Center. Our health is worse than the Third world. Our city at night is a dark and violent money warehouse for rich people up the hill in those fancy towns!

They have turned the city we live in into slave quarters. Slaves need no schools, or recreation, or cultural and social institutions.

Our history and culture is a slum that is periodically destroyed dispersed and hidden in history.

Foreign troops patrol our city streets, the same state troopers who shot us down in 1967 like bloodthirsty stormtroopers.

Like Mobutu bringing Belgian troops into the Congo. Like the U.S. in Saudi Arabia. Or Panama. Or Grenada.

But we are **citizens**. Ha! No, we are being denied citizenship, by denying our self-determination.

We did not elect niggers to do bad—badder—we was already doing that! That's why we was screaming Black Power.

But we got Black middle-class front off and the same even worse oppression, because now they took America out (and it's well-advertised) to the suburbs and left us in the 3rd world, suffering under **neo-colonialism**. As Cabral said, imperialism and white supremacy, does its "ruling through **native agents**."

Black Self-Determination, Self-Respect and Self-Defense are not on Slave Master America's agenda. The corporations have stolen the money, that should have made Black people citizens with equal rights and equal opportunity. They have stolen resources of the richest nation in the world, and invested in restoring the corporate power of Germany and Japan and rebuilding those societies while destroying this one!

Omar's legacy is not just a tragedy of betrayal, it is also a testament to our continuing responsibility.

Hell is a **place**, the **Devil** exists in **human form**!

What other Being would transform Eden into Hades?

Remember, Hell is ruled by **Dis**. We are the tortured slaves of **Dis**!

Disrespected

Discriminated against

Dismissed

Disorganized

murdered to

Disappear

Our children are **dis**appearing

The biggest **Dis** of all!

But let these last words be instructive—like something I could tell Omar, so he would come to understand. That is the spirit we need. Part of the living spirit of Omar that we share and name as part of our collective historical memory.

Let Omar's death live within us as the abiding spirit of promise and sacrifice. It's a reminder of what must be done to change this world. A sacred sign like the rainbow that instructs us that promise is a commitment to struggle as righteous as truth.

That **Hell** is the **submission** to **Evil!**

When you think of Omar think of this:

That any Business in our community should be willing to hire your children. Omar, you, and your friends who need jobs should go in groups to these businesses and see to it!

Any Church in our community should sponsor Day Care and Recreation programs for the whole area and not just for the faithful. The businesses must contribute and help fund these as well.

The Schools must educate our children according to **our real lives** and our real history. They must equip them to help run this city and rebuild it!

Nationally, the descendants of the slaves must have reparations for that enslavement, in the form of **free education** to the highest levels, for all the 244 years of slavery. That many generations must be repaid. Beginning with the 40 million Afro-Americans that now live.

Those negro rulers must be made to become our **servants**, as they pledged when we raised them. Or they must be disempowered and overthrown!

We must begin to treat these Backward Negro Bureaucrats just as we treated the white exploiters. We must fight police lawlessness and racism as we fought them before. We need a Police Review Board!

Instead of the hordes of carpet baggers and scalawags, foreign experts who hold important posts in our city, young Omar, a native son, child of Black activists, should be seated in one of those slick downtown offices, working for us!

In Kenya, Omar is the tragic son of Mau Mau leaders who are now locked up after they led the struggle that destroyed **colonialism!**

Child of Soweto and Panama
A murdered son in Grenada
   or the West Bank
     Dead young brothers
       bleeding in the streets
         actually **wasted by some mad creation** *of this Hell*!

Let our sadness move us to remember we know what to say when we ought to. Let it prompt us to turn our hot anger our hatred of betrayal, conscious as the madness and violence which brought us here, and be focused on the destruction of the unrighteous! Either that or we die, slaves.

Racism is **Nazism** and these **cities** are the **concentration camps!** The **Ghettos!**

Fight Evil or lose your children and your future to torture and tragedy. Stop the War on the Youth!

The purpose of city government and city institutions must be the education, housing, employment, social development and well being of its people! How can people who don't live here, live better by working here, than those of us who live here all our lives?

It can only be slavery, we did not vote to remain poor and exploited.

It can only be betrayal—we thought we had delivered ourselves, that we had made revolution. But now our slavery is maintained by a backward, reactionary, corrupt bureaucratic negro and white middle class who feed on the crumbs, often children's flesh, that fall their way from the greedy slobber of the outright Devil's mouth of B.S. and money.

Gaudy flies crawling on filth. Educated maggots living in corpses. Carriers of pestilence and disease. They live as **proof** of our ignorance! As if we were too primitive to dig that these flies who ride us have given us **The Sleeping Sickness.**

That their bite wastes our youth. That those poisonous insects are the spreaders of this epidemic of frustration violence corruption and murder!

Cry out about this betrayal, about this abandoning of our children to a jungle of violence and wasted lives, killed outright or to live the death slavery is.

In Omar's name, remember and speak! Go in groups, like you were exterminating infestations of poison flies killing your people with sleeping sickness. We would burn them. As a sign of civilization and science.

Remember Omar, his beautiful mother who taught him from infancy to fight against Evil. His father who has regularly fought, rumbled and went upside the Devil's head, upholding justice.

Remember his brothers and sisters who love him, who are also threatened like all our children. Remember their love and loss and connect it with your own, with ours, with your neighbors. Collectively, as sincerely as prayer, speak and act to kill evil before it kills us, our children 1st!

Go in groups, if you stand on corners visit the businesses and churches and schools and police stations in your neighborhood and demand jobs, recreation, day and health care.

In Omar's name. Demand justice and an end to betrayal. And let a whole community of us, whether we follow Jesse Jackson or Louis Farrakhan or Michael Jackson or Public Enemy. Begin now, rebegin now, on the street where you live. Fight for life against death. Use love against hate.

And remember Omar when you do. Let his death make you angry enough to free yourself and save your children's Lives. Remember Omar.

1990

James "Library" Brown (1937-1991)

James "Library" Brown

Brown James, Brown James Brown! This was the way I described the more famous and louder JB. There is also another James Brown in Newark, on WBGO. I call him Radio Brown. As distinguished from Boogaloo Brown. So in Newark we had 3 Brown Jameses we celebrated, Boogaloo Brown, Radio Brown and of course, our swift brother we are gathered here to commemorate, James "Library" Brown.

Yes, that was the way I distinguished the 3 Jameses. But sure, as much as I dig the other 2, Library Brown was my friend and fellow Newark cultural worker.

And I am shaken and consciously weakened by his quick and unexpected exit. He split much too soon for us who knew him, of course, but James Library Brown was not just an intellectual, a reader and scholar, he was an important person to the people of Newark, even to those who could hear his name and think "Papa's Got a Brand New Bag."

Library Brown was the creator of the Black World in the world of the Newark Public Library. It was Library Brown who 1st openly emphasized and began to put together a Black Studies collection at the library. In tune with the whole Black national movement for Self-Determination, Self-Respect, and Self-Defense of the '50s & '60s and early '70s.

Just as we raised the call for Black Studies in the schools. In fact we are still fighting for Black Studies and a multicultural curriculum in the schools, even right here in Newark with our wall to wall Black bureaucrats, but still no comprehensive program of Black Studies (i.e. focused study of the history, culture and lives of the Afro-American people and the Pan-African peoples) exists in our schools. Our children are still being miseducated by white supremacy in textbooks. Perhaps we should use this sad occasion to reannounce our unswerving commitment to see a comprehensive Black and Latino and multicultural curriculum in Newark Schools. I know Library Brown would like that!

But these are Hard Times we going through right now. It's got a root in our continued economic exploitation and racial oppression by the Klan that runs America, as a cluster of Masters' Mansions surrounded by the slave quarters they have turned these cities into as they gave up direct control for indirect rule through native agents.

So that we might win elections in these cities but as the "real Americans" retreated to the suburbs, they would take all wealth with them and leave us to run poverty stricken cities full of unemployment, educationless schools and falling down institutions.

Yet, Brother Library persevered these years to keep the faith of our mass '60s upsurge. He did not abandon his passion for Black literature just because he got a job in the library! That's what he thought he was supposed to do! Just as we thought, when we elected these politicians that resembled us. We thought that they believed those revolutionary chants, like "Black Power" or "Self-Determination, Self-Respect, Self-Defense" or "Culture is a weapon!" they shouted along with us in the '60s.

We believed as Library Brown did by his acts, that "La Luta Continua!"*—"The Struggle Continues!" And that those who had together pledged with us to raise the level of that struggle as a life commitment would do that. The formal opening of the Library's Afro-American Room, largely from James Brown's leadership efforts is proof that Library Brown was true to his word, that indeed he was a man of integrity and vision! But alas, there are too few parallel expressions of public example of a continuing revolutionary practice by those who got better jobs by using our struggle like gasoline for the gas tanks of their soaring careers.

That is why it is so heavy losing James like this, he was the people's advocate, the protector of our history. I know most of my books are in the library, and the other published Black Newark

---

* A Portuguese phrase which Amilcar Cabral adopted in his writings against Portuguese colonization

writers. I know, also, there are none of our books in the Newark School system. I know there is no Newark Musicians series on WBGO, none in Symphony Hall or the Museum. We are the lone major city without an Afro-American museum. We still don't even have a movie theater! And although I have personally advocated the formation of an All-City Newark "Blues and Jazz Band," city-wide youth and professional repertory theater companies. So now the Newark Symphony has formed a city-wide youth orchestra to play European concert music, and let ignorance, disguised as a Negro bureaucrat, still hold our children for Ransome.*

But Library Brown did create an Afro-American room which we must continue to strengthen and expand! Yes, Library Brown has left a legacy of love for the people, willingness to struggle, scholarship and integrity!

We ask publicly today, who will replace him? We must not take Library's replacement lightly! I think Alex Boyd is doing a wonderful job. But I also know that w/o Library Brown's lead of the struggle for a new head librarian we might still have a "real property" expert as Chief Librarian, even lighter than Walter White.

So we must make certain that our new Black Studies librarian is as scholarly and committed to change as Library Brown. Also we must begin to insist that the heads of our institutions and municipal departments be chosen from Newark residents. Of the top cultural institutions and city bureaus' heads most have been brought from outside Newark!

Why? Is it to continue the same lack of opportunity and blunted social mobility we experienced under foreign domination? Newark people must get these jobs. We must create a tradition of raising the level of this city from the inside, not always w/ hired guns and traveling professionals.

Maybe Newark residents cannot get these top jobs because the people who run the city don't want to have anyone around who knows where the skeletons are hidden. No one who has long-time

---

* James Ransome was the Chairman of Newark Public Schools' music departments.

ties in this city. No one who is close to Newark's people, they might want to make change.

Sharpe James don't bring in a hired gunman as Police Director! You should get Charlie Knox and pay him from that money Florio helped the suburbs steal from our kids and our schools.*

The Library is as important as the Police Department. If you don't understand that, it's because you've been trained with the curriculum of continuing slavery, our ghetto socialization.

We must replace Library Brown with an advocate of the people, not one of our enemies' "cannoneers," for whom literature and art are expressions of white supremacy and Black literature and art is some sociological voodoo.

What always made me chuckle when talking to Library Brown is that as quiet and dignified as he was, he had that passion for self-determination born of his commitment and knowledge of truth and history. He could be talking quiet but the ideas were loud as the Black masses demand for Democracy!

But now he is gone. Another friend. Another wonderful personality and creative educated mind. Yet he is gone! Why? Just as a few weeks ago, another close friend and exemplary citizen, Specks Hicks was murdered in our city, yet his killers still walk free! Was that his payment for loving Black people and struggling to raise our community?

So our brother, James Library Brown. Why is he dead? Murdered also, as sure as if it was with a bullet penetrating his body, shot by an assassin's gun.

He is dead because after the Gay Power rebellion in San Francisco in the '70s where a street full of police cars was burned, suddenly there arose the smart bomb disease of AIDS. Why then? If this disease was natural and historical, Alexander the Great and Oscar Wilde, ubiquitous famous personages, should have got it. Certainly their times were less advanced in health and disease prevention technology. Then how come AIDS now? And how come,

---

* Charlie Knox is a lifetime Newark resident who was named police chief by Mayor Kenneth Gibson in his last term. He went on to become head of the New York/New Jersey Port Authority Police.

after it was highlighted as a homosexual disease, suddenly it has gotten as smart as Schwartzkopf's bombs and zeroed in on Black People? Think about it. The U.S. Govt. gave poison blankets to kill the Cherokees. They sterilized 50% of the women in Puerto Rico. They gave Black men syphillis in Alabama as an experiment to see if it would kill them. It did!

No, if you never suspected anything like a conscious conspiracy against us (not counting **chattel slavery**) you must abandon your trained naiveté and regard AIDS as a Malthusian form of imperialist chemical warfare. Malthus was a European philosopher who thought that the world was messed up because there were too many people. This disease is politically more specific, it thinks there are too many Blacks and Gays!

So we must not regard AIDS as simply a Gay disease! It is clearly not Gay at all. It is the mustard gas of our time and the battlefield is our world and it is your color and sexual orientation or your use of intravenous injections or maybe even your job that mark you. Most of the AIDS patients in New Jersey, and Newark is one of the highest concentrations of AIDS, are Black and not Gay, but intravenous users. We must use this occasion to call also for more AIDS research.

The struggle for Black Self-Determination and the struggle for equal rights for all people, regardless of sexual orientation, are both struggles for democracy. We must be part of a conscious United Front to struggle for American People's Democracy against the steady, deadly rise of American fascism rahrahed in by the Ray Gun and explosively propelled by the Bushman.

How soon will the Afro-American room be named something like the James Brown Pan-African Wing or maybe just Library Brown as a major continuing collection of the history, literature and art of Black people in the U.S. and all over the world?

Our celebration and memory of our Library Blood must take the form of making that Black studies collection the best in the state, the best in the East, the best in the West, you know the rest!

Yes, how much Pride and Self-Respect would we have to generate, how much public education, to make the James Brown Collection and the Newark Library the best in the world? So that

people would talk about our Library and the James who made
the Newark Library a righteous Brown! Like that scream his
Brother Boogaloo be doin'! (Wow!) (Sing) Newark Library!
Library Brown! (scream) Wow!

1991

Miles Davis (1926-1991)

When Miles Split!

Someone called me and said you died, Miles. Yeh, that cold. Here in North America, with all the other bullshit we put up with. You know. I know you know. Knew. And still know, wherever you is.

I'm one of yr children, actually, for all the smoke and ignorant mimmy jimmies . . . you know / I can say that. I was one of yr children / you got a buncha children man, more than you probably dug on the serious side. Not innocent ass fans. But the school of the world you created me from inside the world's head. You gotta buncha children brother. I still am. Will be. In some important ways. For instance, I will never take no shit. Yr legacy. I will never believe anybody can tell me shit. Unless they are something I can feel. Like Aretha said. Something I can feel. You were that. I cd feel you, I cd be you when I was a little boy, up the street with the trumpet bag. I wanted to be in that music. I wanted to be that hip, that out, that whatever it was I felt you were. I wanted to be that. All my life.

What it was was the place and the time. But it was you describing it with your feeling. For me that place was Newark, where we grew, and then here you come so hip. I cd dig that I needed to be that, but more, I knew, I was that. I was with you in that fingering, that slick turn and hang of the whole self and horn. And the sound. I had never been in that place, there wasn't no such place in Newark, before.

I mean I never thought of nothing before like *Venus* with *Godchild*. I never thought of nothing before like *Venus De Milo*. There was nothing in my life like that before you brother. And then the persona, what it all spelled. Yeh, I wanted to look like that. That green shirt and rolled up sleeves on *Milestones*. That cap and seersucker on Dig, I always wanted to look like that. And be able to play *Green Dolphin Street* or *Autumn Leaves* or

Walkin or *Blue Haze* or *Round Bout Midnight*, or yeh yeh yeh yeh hey, even the mammy jammin *Surrey With The Fringe On Top*, as whatever he wanted, as tiny lyric, or cooler than thou, hot pointillist funkmares, cubist, expressionist, impressionist, inhabiting your being into a plane of omniscient downness (dig that!)

It was the self of us all the way without anything but our saying, our breath, night times, or walking where we was. We could be whole and separate from any dumb shit. We could be the masters, the artist, the diggenist knowers, the suave, the new, the masters.

This is what art doos. Your voice, that out sharp growl. That was how art should dig itself to be talking. *So What* is probably a prayer in the future.

I held my horn like that, and rolld my body like an ark of music, just looking at things. The cool placement of emotion. The information. I carried that consciously. No one could put me down, I was Miles child. His man. somehow. anyway.

And then each change, stage, was a path I wd walk. When I heard you as a little boy. Then went to see you. You was me alright. You was one of the few I could let be me.

Now some motherfucker wanna tell me you outta here. No. No. Miles. Why? You left? So right away I figure none of the shit still here is cool. But dig, Dizzy and Max is still here. So that's the pain. And I know I dig you. I know I carry *Dr. Jackle* in my speech. And *Godchild* and *Miles Ahead* and *Kinda Blue* and even *Porgy and Bess*, somethin Gershwin cdnt do.

Cause no one was that tender, that touching the where touch cd ultimately is.

They taking all the Giants. You. Trane. Duke. Monk. Billie. Your whole band is dead, man. Paul. Philly Joe. Cannonball. John. Red. Your whole band. And what does that do to us, but leave us on the shore watching the waves, and trying to write music from that regular funk.

But what it says is that our youth is gone. That we are the adult. (What that?) That you have it in yr hand now, to do. That if it will go, this life, this memory and history, this desire for freedom and a world family. That's it's on you.

Like I dug, when Philly Joe hattd up. On us. If we are the ones.

If it is to be, something other than the savages and bush mens. Then we got to. The giants. Our fathers and mothers. Sassy split last year. Monk. Count. LTD. If it is to go then we are the goers. The comers. In that whole sound and thought. That life that makes the blues. Tha makes the dark hip, the roll and rumble. Yeh. Then, if all that long two hundred centuries of slick, is to be on bein. Then we are the only carriers.

I cd dig the way you walked and held that horn. That gorgeous chilling sweet sound. That's the music you wanted playing when you was coming in a joint or just lookin up at the sky w/ yr baby by yo side. That mixture of America and Remerica and them Changes, them blue Africa magic chants. So I am a carrier. I got the stick. I aint stopping. If you, whoever else you tapped, then them too.

Headline the Giants are murdered. Then we got it. All of those who finally must dig, dont say it brother, truth and beauty. But who am I talkin to if you split, Miles, Man, and what the fuck is there to listen to? (OK, Everything!)

Except, you did leave jabillion ultra hip notes, 70 billion swift blue cool phrases. And how many millions of unheard dig'its, them nasty nasty silences right in the middle of the shit. Bee-bee beep beeppp, ba dee da dee da...

So what about it, like they say in the tradition, what about it, is Miles and them, John, Duke, Monk, Sassy all, the giants, does it mean our shit is over with? I know about the records and shit. I'm not talking about that. Does it mean, with the crazies vampin and now even some things look like regular niggers can break out with bushy tongues. Where before with your cool **Boplicity** in our heads it was somehow not only soft yet sharp yet gentle but like a weapon against such square shit as most of the rest of America is. That all of you giant figures that we emulate and listen to and hear and visualize night after night inside our heads, from the nightclubs, the concert halls, the bars, the records, the TV . . . is this, your death, like some hideous omen of our own demise, and I mean everybody here, not just niggers, cause if we go, this whole playhouse go up in smoke.

No, I mean either this death is the beginning of death in cut time, or it means that one earth has turned and another begun. One age, one era, one being. Listening to you now, and knowing that whole of change you went through, from life to life, from music to music, from revelation to revelation, even evolution can be dissolution or devolution.

But you was Bop when you got here, flyin w/ the human headed soul Ba, Bird, the doped up revolutionary. Next, you was Cool. It was like your own creation yet, of course, very Presidential. Then you got with Philly and them for the harder Bop and then got Ball, the Dis Heah and Dat Dere of we funky story. Then you sic'ed the straight out vision monster on us, Trane, in that perfect wonderful all time clasical hydrogen bomb and switch blade band. Let us all always be able to hear *Straight No Chaser* anytime we want to.

I know the last few years I heard you and saw you dressed up all purple and shit, it did scare me. All that loud ass rock and roll I wasnt into most of it, but look brother I heard *Tutu* and *Human Nature* and *D Train*. I heard you one night behind the Apollo for Q, and you was bashin like the you we knew, when you used to stand coiled like a blue note and play everything the world meant, and be in charge of the shit too. I'll always remember you like that Miles, and yr million children will too. With that messed up poppa stoppa voice, I know you looken up right now and sayn (growl) So What?

1991

Ellis B. Haizlip (1929-1991)

The Soul Brother

Back during the '60s peak of Afro-America's most recent revolutionary political upsurge, there was a brother whose very name meant "Soul!" (He used to call me "Imamu", pronounced "E-Mah-Mu".) Brother **Ellis Haizlip**, who has left this tragic hell, who lived with us here in the city of **Dis**, Capital of the devil's thingdom.

We Black folks are like Sisyphus, condemned to roll the huge boulder of white supremacy continuously up the racial mountain, our brother Langston told us about. (Happy birthday, Langston!) He called it "The Negro Artist And The Racial Mountain."

And at each bitter exhausting height to which we finally manage to push it, repeatedly, cruel devils who scream they are Gods! hurl the giant boulder down on us again.

In the 19th-century anti-slavery movement, the '20s Harlem Renaissance, the '60s Civil Rights and Black Liberation Movements, were such thrusts and at each juncture our intensified political struggle produced an art, a revolutionary democratic culture, which was one spearhead and reflection of the political struggle. In the anti-slavery 19th century, it was Douglass, David Walker, Frances Harper—the slave biographers. The '20s Du Bois, Langston, Zora, McKay, &c. The '50s Baldwin, Hansberry. The '60s Larry Neal, Henry Dumas, John Coltrane.

The '60s political advance was reflected and stimulated by a surge of Black attempts at true self-consciousness, national consciousness, cultural revolution.

In this context, Ellis Haizlip's name meant **Soul**. The power of the sun's spirit manifest as feeling, understanding, development! Ellis's program *Soul* was a national Afro-American media institution created by the conscious determination of the Afro-American struggle.

Ellls brought us Black Power activists and progressive Afro-American artists and entertainers; word from the front and information to help protect our backs. He was, in this real sense, a messenger, like an electronic Griot, giving us the griotry of our advanced intentions, our most important concerns.

If James Brown was "Soul Brother number one," Ellis Haizlip was "the Brother be on *Soul*!" In this sense Ellis was very much a significant and well-loved figure in our '60s cultural revolution.

But like the Sisyphus Syndrome which defines our struggle, our jagged rise and fall and rerise and refall, up and down the racial mountain, by the mid-'70s when the Black Liberation Movement had reached one plateau (Malcolm and King murdered, ditto JFK and RFK!), *Soul* was removed from TV, just as many of the gains of the preceding period were and are still being eliminated.

On Channel 13 now, we see Mr. Moyers tell us we are our own worst enemies. Or we can see the Anglophile Eurocentric cultural religious hour, or we might learn that "Creativity began in Greece" from programs called "The Art of The Western World."

Today we can see how backward the times are, racist violence in the streets, imperialist war, Bush vetoing Black civil rights, plunging us back to de jure segregation!

So we are still looking for our Soul to return to the media. Still working on recreating yet again a new movement for Black Self-Determination, Self-Respect and Self-Defense, anti-war and anti-fascism.

So we remember Ellis as we remember the times when we were winning. When revolution was the main trend in the world today! Until a time when we rise again, to the challenge of destroying slavery and white supremacy forever.

Ellis Haizlip, our Soul Brother, in turning completely into spirit on us, reminds us that this task yet confronts us. Like when Ellis said "S O U L" we focused clearly and were strong. (Ellis used to say, "How are you, EE Maah Moo?")

Thank you, Ellis. Brother Soul. For being one messenger of our cultural revolution. And like the rest of us, the sun's child. The fundamental spirit of R (Ra) over R Not. Life against Death. Be with us when we rise again!

Hey, Man
    Check you
        later . . .
    You dig?

                      1991

Specks Hicks (1933-1991)

Specks

All of what I want to say arrives in torrents, of emotion, memory, felt history. Over 40 years of our lives. Specks and those of us who knew him, knew each other. Imagine all the world in between us all, all the space and information. All the experience.

Specks, for me, is part of my own life and history. Like so many of us here today. He already entered American literature formally in the '60s in many of my stories and poems. He was my "Bigger Thomas," the bad brother who could never be whipped down by the criminal insanity of slavery.

He was leader of the Dukes in them old days. In black berets and bomber jackets stalking the blue black gray iron of Newark nights with the clean integrity of a loaded revelation.

Yes, for us, Specks always represented the most sensitive aspect of our environment, as tough and sinister as it was. Still, there was a constancy, a handling of it, that was heroic and asked no quarter, and strode as arrogantly independent as anything on the planet.

Yet, now we are asked to read a newspaper story and be done with him. We are asked to paw over some garbled incomplete information and make some formal summation of his life. If we could do this, we could do it to ourselves, then we would be suicidal. And nothing more would be heard from any of us. Our history could be written by George Bush, and our meaning would be as twisted and untold as the exploding teeth of fire gnawing through the Middle East, so thousands die, our children included, all explained, they tell us, calmly, each time the wind blows and flaps some mindless yellow ribbon.

But Specks Hicks is more than a pile of newspapers, more than a transient story shoved across the city editor's desk. He is part of this community in a deep and touching way. He is part of our historical personality as a city, part of the basic toughness, the savvy, the downness and aggressive seeking of an entire generation. That is why it is so critical that we seek deeply into his murder and be clear and clean and allow no ambiguities or dusty corners of non-telling to obscure what has happened and what it means!

Because whoever killed Specks would kill any one of us or all of us in here! Whoever killed Specks is a grim monster that must, for all of our sakes, be cornered and removed from society. No matter who it is!

I say this because rumors are flying like desert storm. The mob. A loan. Drugs. Undercover work. Knucklehead niggers. All of it is flying. But this cannot end with the titillation of rumors. All of us have something at stake in this. All of our lives are on the line. It is not a coincidence that the entire city has grown grayer and less familiar more alienating, especially as the lie of the Bush Arab massacre gets more clear and people begin to see that each day three or four Hiroshima's were dropped on Iraq.

The message is that this is the murder kingdom. Dis. That we are of no value to the rulers except for killing material. If our own children are so sick that they would do this, then we must stop everything in the street. And turn the schools and jails upside down, transform the relationships to the productive process and make sure that not only are our children properly educated, but that we can benefit by the enormous wealth at our disposal, from our taxes, in this town that is still used up by white suburban colonialism.

If it is knucklehead niggers, petty dope dealers, then that must be dealt with. If these people are going to deal dope in our communities, the same as during prohibition, they must at least build the political and social structures the Irish and Italian and Jewish mobs built and police their own savages. And pay off whoever's got to be paid off. But the neo-fascist police state the rulers use to reoccupy the Black and Latino communities must be eliminated at once!

Moreover, the drug trade should be completely **decriminalized**. The money taken out of the narcotics, so that the unregulated, completely wild big capitalism of the drug business can be contained, the way cigarettes and liquor are. And drugs decriminalized the same way liquor was. Please, never believe for one moment, that those little Black "chilly home boys" with their hats turned around to the side with the eight ball jackets are the real profiteers of drugs! I know everybody in here knows better than that!

If Specks's assassination is political or the mob, then we must with equal determination and equal thoroughness find it out, and punish whoever has done it. No matter who it is, no matter what level of government or mobocracy, they must be punished and locked up or mailed to the next planet.

Why? Because we will not have it. We will not stand for it. You cannot kill Specks and get away with it. We are not punks! Whoever killed Specks, we must bring in, dead or alive, however you can. Drop a dime, pull a trigger, run the suckers over with a car. Whatever. This must be done.

In a time when the very recent colonialists of Mozambique and Angola tell us, in our own city, that we discriminate against them, and the opium of the people is a Bush man who sends our children to die after vetoing their civil rights. When animals begin to put up pro-slavery racial signs again, and say it is legal for us to be called names again, even on college campuses and even attack Black people on the street, as often as not murdering them, as if we were nothing. In this reactionary period when each week another colored pod from out of the white supremacy factory pops up to tell us it is all our fault. It seems our human esteem has gotten so low, or the white supremacy ghouls, in this land we created with our labor, are so inebriated with the disorganization of our freedom movement, or the patriotic "Butelezihood" of new or at least contemporary captivity planned for us, that they feel they can kill our leading citizens and get away with it.

But it ain't like that, suckas. The mayor, police chief, county, state, individual police, regular citizens, businessmen, professionals, hustlers, sportsman, intellectuals, we must track down this murderer or murderers any way we can. To kill Specks, an honored citizen of this community, a Black man we loved and looked up to, admired, for whatever reason, is impermissible. It besmirches the name of our city and makes us look like ignorant punks. It is an insult, a dis, that is, disrespect, an insult, we must not permit.

When Mhisani, Harold Wilson, another one of our community working class heroes, was murdered mysteriously, a few years ago, apparently shot by some stick-up men on Avon Ave., there was a big uproar, momentarily, but what happened? Much cover up and side stepping, but when will we be men and women? When will we admit what we need to live and insist on it before the world and swear to re-create our lives as such or as the old song says, "Before I be a slave I'll be buried in my grave."

Yes, it means that much. Think about it. Try to feel it with me, so you understand. Specks meant something. He was something real in our collective psyche, not only to us, subjectively, but objectively.

In the 1970 transfer of power to a neo-colonial deferral of our rights, the middle-class Negro ascended to some false hegemony, but no one should doubt the real power is the peoples' when we discover how to actually take it. And the **advanced working class**, such as Specks, those working people, who through the dint of their own work and curiosity turn themselves into intellectuals and begin to understand the society thoroughly and take those principled positions in it, must be valued by us. They should be even more highly valued than they are now, because don't they represent the path the majority of us must take to finally understand where we are in Dis, the capital of Satan's kingdom, and finally do something about it?

I mean, that whoever killed Specks should have been afraid to, should not even have ever considered it, were we as strong as we need to be to resist the war and fascism and new wave of corruption and white supremacy that is coming our way.

I can name brothers, Walter Koontz, Mhisani, Nsongi, Kamiel Wadud, Paul Nakawa, from this town all gone, very young, the best of a generation. The most conscious, the most committed to social transformation, the most fit to pursue its activist demands. Yet they are dead. All mysteriously, most violently or suddenly!

And more than this I can name, from right here in this community, shot out on the pipe, set up, locked up, shut up, intimidated, compromised, sold out, whatever, so that old slavery goes on, in its varied ways.

We even have Negroes, on the loose, reemerged from the Negro laboratories the slave masters keep under the undertakers' offices, where they manufacture Negroes to crawl around beggin', tryin' to ignorant us to death. At St. J.'s, a ghost Negro tells us Specks cannot be buried there, and we are clear at least on the difference between the babbling house Negro, some of whom might even go to this church, and the Negro who actually owned slaves!

But I take Specks's death like this, so let this be a coat puller. We are here in this city of our collective lives, struggle and history. As the U.S. moves further and further toward fascism, and the triumph of white supremacy, for the international imperialist order upon which it is based, we Black folks in the cities will find ourselves increasingly distanced and alienated from the federal government.

In their supposed slickness, Bush like Reagan and the reactionaries before him have tried to initiate a repositioning of a kind of **states' rights**, where because the cities have gotten so Black and politically organized, **the slave masters will now control us from the state level.**

Even the peoples' supposed victory in the *Abbott vs. Burke* education ruling where we were to get more money for education to offset the reality that the Black cities are poorer than the white suburbs has now been turned around by the marshaling of the reactionary racist suburbs (A Lynch Mob) to steal our money to lower their taxes, while every day coming into these cities taking most of that and the money out.

We must begin to see that the only way we can move, survive and develop is to pass laws continuously confirming the democratic control of the cities. That these cities will continue to be even mightier fortresses against the heathenism of fascism and white supremacy like our law outlawing the Klan in Newark, or banning South African imports or corporate collaboration.

We must pass laws in this city, making racism a punishable crime. Even as Bush tries to make it the new state religion, nationally. We must legislate new governmental citizen social and economic relations to put citizens in more direct access to the wealth of our tax dollars, new jobs in the public sector. We must make the public sector strong and use it to rebuild the entire infrastructure and self-reliance of these cities. So that they can be city states against the new world order of Emperor Bush and the money manager murderers.

And I say this as if I stood here in a tan English-plaid double-breasted suit, with stacy and adams, a gold watch, and of course, the laid back what's happenin' tilt of the smoothly perfect lid, framing the historic glasses, under and through which ease the warmest chuckle of digging, as if love had certain manners, was cool and measured in its steady appearance, to circle all the things we could remember that made us happy and name names and new ideas we got, some we still keep and treasure like our own names.

Yes, there has been so much motion in all our lives, for Specks it was not just the cutting loose of the Vanz*, the dope, now many years ago, before it got so famous, when Specks was one of the only soldiers in the real war on drugs, not the one fought by profiteers like Fair Oaks** which charge $1,400 a day.

From the jump, Specks knew skag was a state introduced neo-slavery. But he nixed that and even got respectable waging that fight. He became a more political figure, even a city official, always clean as daylight.

Carrying himself the way we all, in some way, must. Alert, proud, wise, in motion, working for change, straight and dignified, yet syncopated with the hipness of close understanding of where he was and what was going on! That is, in tune with the life of the living culture of the people he was.

So who raised a hand against us all, through Specks? Who would try to kill our best memory of ourselves as wise courageous heroes?

---

* Vanz (heroin)
** Fair Oaks (a private rehabilitation clinic)

We would always, everywhere, be as bad as we had to be, to hang out with you, Specks. You were part of the ammunition of our socialization in this city of sidewalks and corners. No matter where we went or were we always carried you with us brother, like, No, no one don't mess with us, not even them squares with the iced up ears. It was that too, we would never submit to no kind of chumped off Henry Cupcake life even flung from the lower middle class, we grew up on these streets where the Black working class ran it on the deep feeling side just like the music. And Specks was one of my models, whether college Negroes, Air Force sergeants, New York pretend intellectuals, or the oppressor state. No! You don't violate us, never, not even in a joke. Specks was part of our social conscience part of the best image of ourselves, part of the reality and lore of our sacredly guarded true self consciousness.

Let us all in here today, who mean well, who are sensitive to the dimensions of real life and meaning below all the surface noise, let us here today make a collective pact, that in whatever way we can, whether major or minute, that we will help to track down our friend's murderers. It is the only way we can keep on hanging out with Specks, and carry ourselves with some respect.

1991

Jimmy Anderson (1932-1988)

July 11, 1992

Jimmy Anderson, friend, brother, artist, great musician, composer, bon vivant, raconteur. He of the big round sound, and big round mind. Jimmy and I had a couple of gambits we used to run on each other. Routines. Like one, I had a pencil with a miniature light bulb on the end of it. The joke was, if you stuck it in somebody's ear and it didn't light up, they was dead daid dead.

One night, we discussed the thumb as the critical tool of human development. The twisted toe that came to be the tool maker. Like the animal sounds, at the same time, became articulated, into vowels and words. The same time as the broke toe got evolved into a thumb. So the thumb was the key symbol of human development. Jimmy would come in some nights and I'd say, "What's happening, Jimmy," and if things was bad he'd hold up four fingers with the thumb bent over hidden, to say it's hard hard hard out here, aint no humanity too tough going on. And we'd break up. Sometimes, it would be some folk or another who would get so thoroughly out that Jimmy would hold up the four finger sign. You know. Signifying Monkey style.

But the deepest connection Jimmy and I had was the music. I remember we used to sit and talk about Ellington for hours, and I'd put on the sides. Ellington, all five fingers of both hands. Or we might listen to Trane. You could hear Jimmy running it back downstairs at *Kimako's** many nights. I remember he and Leo Johnson did unaccompanied duets one night. Took everybody out.

One of our constant conversations though, was the arts here in Newark. What could be done? To force this development. To get the arts where they belonged. In the schools, the churches, the

---

*The arts space of Amina and Amiri Baraka

157

vacant lots, the parks, the cultural institutions. Because Jimmy and I knew the essence of art is life, and love or revelation.

I tried to get the city fathers to put Jimmy's book on teaching improvisation in the schools but nothing happened. I tried to get them to consider Jimmy as head of the music dept. in the public school. So perhaps we could at least hear some of the classics at these graduations instead of second-rate everything.

We knew that one key to the people's development was the confrontation with the classic arts of the culture. That inside that music, for instance, was the history of the people. That listening to Billie Holiday singing *God Bless The Child* would teach you as much about U.S. society as any social studies class. That Duke's *Black Brown and Beige* would teach you more history than most of these classrooms. But how to do it.

A brother like Jimmy, with so much talent, yet relatively so little recognition, makes you think, how can our children and our people advance if their most advanced thinkers and image makers are kept away from them? But how can education be real without them without art without the history contained in it, the experience and information?

But we knew that finally it was up to us. The artists themselves. We had to go out and bring the word, the sounds, the images to the people. That we could not just walk around putting people down for not giving us work, when we were the first persons to say these powers that be were bankrupt mediocre and corny. Jimmy would hold up his four fingers. Hey man, he'd say, put that pencil in that dude's ear and you'll see what's happening.

But this remains of all our talks. That will to do. That will to remain with the people, to be in the community, to speak with the real voice, of five fingers on each hand. To articulate and explain, to move, and to educate, to inspire and change. These were our resolutions, some of our principles.

Where are our All City Jazz Band and All City Drama Company for the schools? Why don't we give letters for poetry and jazz band in the schools? Why isn't the Krueger Mansion becoming an Afro-American museum? What has happened to the Coast project just in front of symphony hall, the old site of the black entertainment district in Newark? Why is it left to rot, while $300,000,000 will be spent to build a Lincoln center downtown, which will no doubt drain all moneys from our Carnegie Hall here, Symphony Hall. We cannot let them destroy Symphony Hall.

We need artists in residence in all the schools. We need an artist in residence to build an artistic culture in this city of rich cultures and history. The arts are not peripheral to human development but at the center of it. Great artists live and die in this city with no recognition. I pity Sarah Vaughan and Wayne Shorter if they did not leave Newark for recognition. Great musicians like Herbie Morgan, Gene Phipps, Grachan Moncur, John Patton, Leo Johnson, Robert Banks, and so many others are here, but who recognizes it? They are education, information, inspiration and economic development, if someone would but recognize it. All these clubs and churches are sites for music or poetry readings or drama. It's up to us, the artists, to take up the challenge, and not leave it to the bureaucrats with social studies degrees. If art is to raise the people, the artists must take it upon themselves.

At *Kimako's*, we are taking up that challenge. This is the pledge we have made, and now make again at this program for bad Jimmy Anderson, our friend, our brother, our comrade in struggle.

1986

Louise Gray (1971-1992)

Louise Gray

In a movie made during the '60s called *The Education of Sonny Carson*, which I advise all of you to get from the video store and look at, for the first time, or look at again, there is a scene much like this one. Where young Black people have clashed and fought and someone has died—the preacher at the funeral asks and repeats this critical question. He says: "Who killed little boy?" He repeats it again and again. "Who killed little boy?"

But today we must change that phrase to "Who killed little girl?" or "What killed little girl?" And no matter the names and faces that might come to mind, we must leave here remembering that the who that killed the little girl, little Louise, 21 years old, just barely reached young adulthood, but not long enough to completely understand it, little Louise, who already had a child, like so many of our children, yet she already had to walk and talk and carry herself like an adult, because her life, our lives, our world had made it so.

When we say, "Who killed the little girl? Who killed Louise?" we must answer, we all killed her, all of us together. Why would we say that, we have not struck the blow, we have not felled this beautiful young child, already with a child. A child that already, at her death, leaves another child without a mother, and another mother without a child. Who killed Louise, yes, we killed her because we continue to live in a jungle and will not look each other in the eye, will not take each other by the hand, will not turn and face the world's enemies, yes, the world's enemies, and move together as brothers and sisters and crush them all forever into dust. Instead we watch as this poor little girl is ripped and broken into dust.

And this is so cruel, because her mother Rosa Gray who I have known for 30 years, herself has never turned the other cheek, or refused to face the great beast that owns our lives, Rosa Gray and Dickie have never taken a step back, have never backed up away from the great beast that brought all our Black selves across the water to slavery. Yet almost like the payback of the evil being himself, now these two strong engaged activist parents are dealt another horrible blow. 1st Omar two years ago, gunned down in these mean streets, and now young Louise. And still we must ask, who killed the little girl, who killed Louise Gray.

And I answer again, all of us, because there are those who have created these mean streets, those who profit from our slavery, yes, I call it that, because it is slavery still. Because whoever lacks self-determination lacks democracy, and whoever lacks democracy is little more than a slave.

I say we lack, we Black people, we Afro-Americans, we lack self-determination, because look at us, how we live, most of us, how we have to make a living, look at our poor housing, our jungle neighborhoods infested with junkies and dope dealers and muggers and killer cops. We did not vote for this. No one ever came to us and said do you want to live like most Americans or do you want to live in the slums, you want to live in clean healthy neighborhoods with good schools, like in the rest of America, or do you want to live in the ghetto? In fact, we're not even in America, on the real side, we live somewhere in the violent neo-colonies of the 3rd world. Now, no longer ruled by foreign domination, like the classic colonies, but now ruled by native agents, that is, people who look like ourselves, but we're still ruled, still dominated, by a small class of well-to-do folks, now fronted by a small class of middle-class Negroes, while the rest of us suffer in poverty, poor education, poor health care, and barely, if at all, employed.

Unlike most Americans, we were brought here as slaves. On our backs, in the dark, in slave ships. We didn't come here through Ellis Island. That's not our story. We came here as slaves. We never wanted to come. And when old chattel slavery came to an end, before any 13th, 14th and 15th amendments got passed, there should have been a referendum held among Black people where we could vote. On what? **On what should be our relationship to the United States?** Do we want to be second-class citizens, which is no citizen at all? Do we want independence, regional autonomy, federation, there are many many relationships. But that is one of our problems, we think we are citizens, yet we have nothing the citizens have. Go up the hill there past into Livingston and Short Hills, or Morristown, you see it on television, how the citizens live. But not us. The citizens live in decent houses, the citizens are employed, the citizens have health care, the citizens have quality schools, but not us. Why? Because we have neither equal rights nor Self-Determination. And we have stopped fighting for it!

That's why I asked, "Who killed the little girl? Who killed Louise?" You know who did it if you are not too crazy to think. These slave masters who own these ghettoes. These black and white Frankenstein monster cops who patrol these ghettoes like the old "paterrollers" on the plantations. All those who make profit on our tragedy. All those who have sworn to protect us, all those we gave our trust to some years ago when finally we got political leadership that looked like us, yet our lives have not changed, in some cases they have even gotten worse.

Rosa and Dickie Gray fought to get rid of foreign domination. They fought, they got out in the streets, and marched and clawed and screamed and worked the polls and walked the streets to bring some change, and what has it got them? Two of their children murdered in these foul streets, yet our political leaders—colored ones—forget the white ones, Bush is a fascist, "our" political leaders sit in Barcelona watching the Olympics while another child is murdered.

And who killed the little girl, not only this system of economic exploitation and enforced ignorance and national oppression yes, for certain, these conditions, these streets, this damned society of white supremacy and Black repression.

But let this sink in, we killed her too if we do nothing but go along with this foul system. If we mouth the same anti-Black words, go along with the same anti-human social relations. If we do not raise our hands to strike down our enemies, then we are their allies.

We see every day our people confused, betrayed, left out. We see every day our people fighting each other. Like this horrible scene today. Our children fighting each other. Killing each other. But we will not turn around and collectively fight our enemies. We fight each other but we will not fight our enemies.

You youth, you should be organizing yourselves, not to strike each other down. You should take those same large groups of youth and visit these stores and churches and institutions in your neighborhoods, in our cities and demand jobs! If you want to move around the city in large groups, organize those groups to go into these large corporations and demand employment.

If you want to put together large militant organizations, do it, but have those youth groups visit these politicians and demand that they begin to get jobs for our people and housing. Take those large groups to the housing authority to find out why they haven't renovated housing. Why there is no new housing. Take those large groups and go to the Board of Education and demand a thorough and efficient education, new school buildings with books and a multicultural curriculum. Yes, there is a need for large organized groups of youth, but not to help the devil kill you off, but to force those in power to move, to do what they have sworn to do and lied.

Take those large groups into these churches and find out why God and Jesus and them only exist on Sunday mornings but by Monday have left town on the first thing smoking. Find out if they can join in creating employment, recreation, education for you, for all our youth. See why there's no day care centers. Yes, we need large organized, and I repeat that, organized groups to move around the city and visit these corporations, institutions, colleges, churches, politicians, small businesses and find out why we are living in hell, while they live in heaven.

Because until we do that, until we have organized ourselves to seek democracy and self-determination, to change our day-to-day everyday lives, we will be in hell. We will be fed upon by cannibals and bushmen. As long as we stumble along in the Democratic or Republican party and will not organize ourselves to feed, clothe and shelter ourselves, to educate ourselves and take care of and nurture and educate our children, then when we say, who killed the little girl, we will have to raise our hands too. Because if we have not organized and struggled to change this jungle, it will remain a jungle, getting worse and worse each year and one by one it will claim our youth, it will swallow them up and we will all be lost in the belly of this beast.

LET US ALL SWEAR THIS MORNING THAT WE WILL BEGIN AGAIN. THAT WE WILL BEGIN TO ORGANIZE OUR-SELVES NOT TO KILL OUR NEIGHBORS, NOT TO HELP THE BEAST KILL OUR BROTHERS AND SISTERS, BUT THAT WE WILL ORGANIZE OURSELVES TO CHANGE OUR LIVES, TO GET RID OF THIS JUNGLE RULED OVER BY A BUSHMAN AND BEGIN TO PRACTICE LIVES OF SELF DETERMINATION. THAT IS THE ONLY REVENGE WE CAN EVER GET. JUSTICE IS THE ONLY REVENGE! GOOD BYE LOUISE, REST IN PEACE. WE WILL REMEMBER YOU IN OUR STRUGGLES.

1992

John Birks "Dizzy" Gillespie (1917-1993)

Diz

I was into the Orioles, Ruth Brown, Larry Darnell, Louie Jordan, The Ravens, Ya know, the late '40s, just going into high school. When my 1st cousin, George, let me have his older brother Sonny's BeBop collection!

I got those old Guilds, Manors, Savoys and a whole world unfolded before me, beginning with the names: Dizzy Gillespie. Thelonius Monk, Charlie Yardbird Parker. The names, Bud Powell, Max Roach, Klook, Kenny Clarke. The names, the language, another world had opened.

Oop Bop sha Bam (a koo koo mop!) the language, another world. The Land of Ooo Blah Dee. Me and Joe Carroll went there and hung until they sicked Dooie Blah and Dooie Blee on us. Swing Low Sweet Cadillac. (Didn't one of them dudes in the horn section answer after . . . wadie wadie wadie wadie . . . yo wambo . . . YO MAM-OO")

And from the beginning of my entrance into that world, it was Diz who was the central figure, the beckoner, sitting there looking out at me from Esquire, the beret and hornrimmed BeBop glasses. "To Be Or Not To Bop," the caption said, and called him "Diz, The High Priest of BeBop." And that was it for me, then. All the wild stuff they sd about Diz, trying to make you think this or that, escaped me. What I saw was my leader. The twinkle behind the rims, I thought I understood what he was signifying. That's what Diz taught, fundamentally, how to nut out on the square world. That word, Hip! That was with it too, from the beginning. They, and I got in it too, were Hip, Hip cats. Cats. I rather be a cat than a dog, right now!

The Square versus The Hip, and I never forgot that. Even now in this square and ugly world, to be hip in a square world, would make some square call you dizzy.

The Ethiopians called the Pyramid, "the angle of success." They called the Square, "the angle of failure." The cultural continuum even across the middle passage. Like

Oop shoobee doobee
   Oop Oop
Oop shoobee doobee
   Oop Oop!   You Dig?

"A lovers' conversation." In Kush or Nights in Tunisia or approaching Tin Tin Deo. We could also dig the funk of burning Manteca! Dug the circle as

          the whirl
         O world
      the pyramid as
      the rising focus
      of endless energy. I
      and I.
         So the square, goes
      no where. Like the box
      we in. It might rock but
      it sure can't roll (censored censored
      censored censored censored censored censored)
      no matter how high it go
      it always resemble its lowest self

And I went to work then, trying to find out what was really happening. That language too. What's Happening? I had gotten Max Roach & His BeBop Boys. Charlie Parker and his Reboppers. Stan Getz. *Opus De Bop*. *Thriving on a Riff*. I copped Bird's *Repetition*, w/ Strings. Wow.

The titles of the songs drew me in further. They were so . . . yeh, weird. Then I dug the real high priest, in shades and another tam, looking past all of us, into the hipnopocity of everything. Monk. Diz was the leader. The speaker. The political cadre, pushing the music by his playing, by his Dizness. He was His Royal Dizziness. Monk, on the other hand, was inside the deepness, the heaviness of what it was. He made no statements, no daunting alarums (yeh), he was the High Priest, but Diz was royalty.

And Diz titles always carried you somewhere up the street and around the corner where the hip shit was. *Tin Tin Deo*. *The Champ* were two of my 1st self reliant purchases. Now I was in high school and cd get an after-school gig.

A Night in Tunisia, *Kush*, *Con Alma*, and with the Ooo Bop Sha Bams and then Woody Herman's *Lemon Drop*, and Babs' 3 Bips and a Bop, the language of BeBop became easily my own, and still, to this day, remains.

Diz BeBop. The beret, Bop glasses, and a goatee, don't forget that. For a couple of decades journalists around the world would sum up the music, or make cracks about it, using that stereotype of early Diz. Bopper jokes became the norm, for alluding to the crazy, the wild, the frantic. And that's what they called us, because that's what we said.

The language registered our psychological expressions of our social life (and the U.S.'s). We were "wild," "crazy," "frantic," as opposed to trained, nor/mal, static, like regular bourgeois culture.

It was an emotional expression of the common psychological development of urban Afro-America. But that language was a shower of new images. Diz and Bird and Monk and Max and Klook and Bud. *Un Poco Loco* was what Bud said and everybody thought that's what Bop was: craziness.

But like the Zen masters knew, inside Diz's laughter was an absolute rationality, as to How corny this bullshit white face slavery exploiting society was. Is. We needed Diz's assurance that it all could be laughed at. And if you wadn't doing anything else, you least needed to do that. Dig?

Dig? The language. Like Thelonius, you dig? It scrambled me, shot some disparate colors into my mind, trying to make me understand some stuff I needed to, to grow. Things, feeling, revelations, my own acts. That I was entering a higher intellectual culture, in which art was validated as personal experience.

"To Be Or Not To Bop." But Diz was already Bopping. He & Bird, Bud, Monk, KIook, then Max, Miles had created it, as a new speech, a new song. Like a dialectical expression of the new feeling the times demanded, in contrast to the careful dead arrangements the corporations had co-opted swing into.

Where the big classic swinging jazz orchestras had created a fresh expanded contemporary form for Afro-American music. But soon the big band became a commercial and artistic jail, as it was subsumed by the commercial, largely white, "swing" (as a noun) bands. Like '60s jazz was co-opted by fusion.

Diz and the others had worked the big classic bands. Teddy Hill, Lionel Hampton, Errol Hines, Cab Calloway &c. After working those gigs, Diz, Bird and the others would wind up uptown in Harlem, after hours, in Minton's and Monroe's Uptown House, the Black laboratories of sound, the smoke and whiskey academies of soul, where they gave a new generation their self-consciousness.

The bullet sharp experimentation in wailing, the sound's language. To get the blues back into the music, to get the polyrhythms of Africa back, to get improvisation back, as primary, these were the essence of their experiments. To get away from the deadly charts of commercial swing. The tin pan alley plantations.

This was one of the catalysts for Bird and Diz and the young boppers beginning to improvise off the harmonic structure, the chords, of clichéd standards, rather than play those tired melodies.

And those terrible groups that came out of that. Diz, Bird, Klook, Blakey, Max, Miles, Bud, Monk. It was blazing and, yes, weird. That was an acknowledged constant. Frantic. Yeh, we called it that. We was trying to get frantic, trying to get away from Kay Kayser and Sammy Kay. The music turned us on. And it was already Gone, if you dug it!

Our language told where we was coming from and where we was trying to go. Frantic, Crazy, Wild, Out, Gone! We was hip not square. We walked that way, the bop walk, used to dance the bop, these squares talking about you couldn't dance to it. Shit, we danced to all of Diz's shit. We were Boppers. My father even asked me Why I wanted To Be A Bopper. You mean, why did I want to be conscious??

But Diz always held the paramount stature in the music. Bird was the great innovator and genius. But Diz was the leader of the whole shit. Of everybody. The speech and the song. The music and the lifestyle.

Plus, from the beginning, Diz himself was a musical innovator of great impact. He was a theoretician, a teacher, a performer, a composer, an incredible instrumentalist. Dig, of the two U.S. world ambassadors, they choose Louis and Diz, both the same kind of bloods. Both great musicians and great communicators. No matter how jive and bloody the U.S. would be, here come Louie and Diz, and like Louis said, "I'm the real ambassador!!" Nobody could put them down. They were loved around the world.

Dizzy's groups have always been signal. His big bands among the most innovative in the music. Like Diz said when he signed my copy of *To Be Or Not To Bop*, "For My Idol" . . . Hahaha. That's the kind of ambassador Diz was. He was one of my largest culture heroes. And so he rewards me with assuming my regard for him. Incredible.

But the lames always purposely misread Diz, being Lames. They confused his domination over squareness as lack of seriousness. To be serious about squares one needs a gun. But in his autobiography, Diz says his hero was Paul Robeson. In the '40's there was a whole group of Black youth, who called themselves the Paul Robeson movement. And Diz was undoubtedly part of that.

In the '40s, the WW2 made it seem, again, like there might be equality in the offing. There was a social consciousness movement that swept through the Black arts as it had done in the '20s and again in the '60s.

It was the worldwide resistance to fascism that had undergirded it. So that the music, Bop, was also a conscious attempt to tear away from the grim corporate establishment that locked the music up, just as it did the people.

I have always thought Bop language, "Ooo shoobie doobie oop ooo OO shoobie doobie oo oop," for instance, was an attempt to respeak African language. Like the unknown tongue, the African language still glued in our consciousness with our culture. The scatting (which Louis raised earlier!) and the Bop talk that Diz brought, both were attempts to put the instrumental language back into vocal language, and that unknown language of the Black unconsciousness was and is "African" or Afro-American.

Diz was always into Africa. As the titles of his compositions attest to (*Tunisia*, *Kush*, &c.). Diz also hooked up the Pan-American funk to its African origins. Diz was the one who set out the larger expression of what was to be called Afro-Cuban music.

It's internationalist focus is unmistakable. Diz hooked up with Mario Bauza, Chano Pozo, Candido, Machito, Mongo Santamaria, and other great Latin American musicians to reconstruct a new Afro-Latin sound. Called Afro-Cuban music. What Jelly Roll alluded to as "The Latin tinge," Diz brought all the way into full sight. Bringing both the Latino and English Caribbean into focus in Afro-American music. Manteca is a classic, as is the still not well-known *Cubana Be and Cubana Bop*.

Years later, Diz came back from Brazil with what the commercial people tagged "Bossa Nova," again linking the Brazilian Samba with Afro-American jazz.

Now it's too weird to think that even Diz is gone. Almost all the others of that generation have booked. Only the great Max Roach of the original funkateers remains. And a few of the close communers, Sonny Rollins, Roy Haynes, who were younger and among the first disciples. But where there was a deep deep sadness for all the departed. Bird, Bud, Klook, Monk, Miles, like part of myself had left, certainly my youth, and the bright unshakeable hopes of my generation. With Diz's departure, there is not only a sadness, still not completely raised. (I mean, I don't know whether I even believe it yet. Diz might be jivin', he might just pop up somewhere. I heard Jon Faddis play the other day at St. John the Divine and I thought maybe Diz was somewhere cracking up.) But with Diz gone, it's like you don't even feel safe around here no more. Really, like you don't even feel safe!

1993

Sun Ra (1914?-1993)

Sun Ra

I passed through Ra's orbit when they 1st arrived from Chicago into the Loisaida (pre-Latino street signs), early '60s. They swept in, with tales and a frantic grapevine, of every which observation.

The Weirdness, Outness, Way Outness, Otherness, was immediate. Some space metaphysical philosophical surrealistic bop funk.

Some blue pyramid home nigger southern different color meaning hip shit. Ra. Sun Ra.

Then they put on weird clothes, space helmets, robes, flowing capes. They did rituals, played in rituals, evoked lost civilizations, used strangeness to teach us open feeling as intelligence.

In those cellars & lofts, Sun Ra spun a cosmic metaphor. He was a philosopher/musician. He used music as language, and image.

His was a historical music. He began, himself, even before he played alternate piano in Fletcher Henderson's orchestra, when Fletcher conducted. In recent years he even brought Fletcher and Duke back with a sweetness and contemporary restatement that was thrilling.

Ra was so far out because he had the true self consciousness of the Afro-American intellectual artist revolutionary. He knew our historic ideology and sociopolitical consciousness was **freedom**. It is an aesthetic and social dynamic. We think it is good and beautiful!

Sun Ra's consistent statement, musically and spoken, is that this is a primitive world. Its practices, beliefs, religions, are uneducated, unenlightened, savage, destructive, already in the past.

That's why Ra left and returned only to say he left. Into the Future. Into Space. He played *Interplanetary Music*. He described *Angels & Demons At Play*. From his *Heliocentric* vision, Ra's music unfolded, it was always, it seemed, always there. What it was. But it let us go into it further, showed us its multiple shapes, its wholeness.

Ra was at the Black Arts, in Harlem, the 1st program we had. He was always up there with us. Talking. Playing. He was one of the presences preaching expanding Black consciousness, as expanding human consciousness. The Sphinx is half human half animal. It rises in fire as the human soul, BA, the Black Bird.

It was Sun Ra and The Myth Science Arkestra that marched across 125th St. with us the day the Arts opened, in Harlem, announcing the '60s cultural revolution and sparking a Black Arts Movement, Poetry, Theater, Music, that complemented the Malcolm X-inspired rise of the new SNCC, Panthers, RNA, CAP, YOBU and the insurrectionary phase of the Black Liberation Movement.

It was Ra, those weekday evenings at the BARTS, who introduced the so called "Light Show" the rockers ripped off. With his "Space Organ" and its Pythagorean connection of Sound to Color. A low note a dark hue. A high note a bright color. Flashed into the dark theater from Ra's miraculous Space Organ.

Ra was also the pioneer in using various then-weird electronic instruments. But he used everything. You could characterize one aspect of his music as African, as Indian, Latino, Caribbean, but it was all that as Afro-American jazz.

No matter how "far out" the insiders said Ra was, in the Harlem streets he was a rare treat. Likewise on Stirling Street, Newark, in a vacant lot up the street from our Spirit House, Ra brought a huge crowd one summer. And we bathed and luxuriated in the swelling twilight funk. Like we were stretched from here to **anythere**.

We brought the Arkestra back later for a Mardi Gras that *Kimako's Blues* people put on. "What you gonna do when they push that button?" they chanted, marching up Branford Place up onto a flatbed truck on Broad St.

"Kiss your ass, Kiss your ass, Kiss your ass, Goodbye." The long screaming chord by the whole Arkestra had stopped people in their tracks. Like an encounter of the further than 3rd type.

"What you gonna do when they push that Button? Kiss your ass Goodbye!"

At times Ra and his Cosmocentric or Heliocentric or Myth Science or Omniverse Arkestras would raise its music as an expression of strange ritual drama. There were Space Goddesses, June Tyson, Verta Mae Grosvenor, who strode through the music in dances of forgotten language. Expressing the ancient continuum of religion and ritual drama.

That was a fundamental expression of Ra's music, a communal consciousness, describing the life before Babel and its mindless tower, as well as prophesying its coming.

The Arkestra was a family, whose life was music, a life of philosophy. But many giants moved through it, but there were giants who remained.

Pat Patrick, the great baritonist and multi-reed hipster, was my very good friend. People always told us we looked alike, which was funny to us, even if it was true.

John Gilmore, I have always thought, is one of the finest and hippest tenor players I know. Plus, I have known John since I met Ra. John is always on it, into Another Kind of signification and expression.

It's **true**, Trane did cop from John Gilmore. Trane would be the 1st to tell you that too. He told Gilmore.

Marshall Allen, a giant. There is no alto saxophonist I know today, or generally, hipper than Marshall. That this is not common knowledge is depressing.

Sun Ra did the music on a record I produced of my play *A Black Mass*, a retelling of Elijah Muhammad's telling of the myth of Jacoub, the mad Black magician who created white people!

After the Newark Mardi Gras, Ra came up to the house, it was a block party, in and out of our basement theater, *Kimako's Blues People*. Ra held court, in front of a spectacular spread of classic Afro-American cuisine Amina had prepared. A bottle of Courvoisier, diverse friends.

Like the grand salons of advanced civilizations, where philosophers and intellectuals and artists could hold forth in open pleasurable serious discussion about the whole world and profound reality.

There was in Ra and continues in his music, the witness of alternatives to all of this and what it's got going on. The evolution of humanity was his theme. From revelation to revelation, immeasureable, revolution to revolution, like heartbeats of truth. The breathing of always.

"We Travel The Space Ways," in that beautiful harmony as song chant, spiritual and scientific. Our bodies, our minds, our worlds, our consciousness, what is, travels the spaceways.

"From planet to planet." Perhaps earth will be evacuated, as Welles and Azimov and Bradbury wrote. The environmentalists could explain.

But also, the tower, the to where? The destiny, but as a constant character of motion and change. When?

We are the creators of Heaven and Hell. Everything you imagine has already been done and can be done. What you can't even imagine is where Sun Ra begins.

The possible is obvious, what is desired and described, is the **impossible**.

What is not is what drives what is, and transforms it into itself. What is becomes what is not and what is not becomes what is and what is not.

The Future is always here in the past.

"Next stop, Jupiter!"

1993

Charlie James Richardson (1928-1993)

Bad News

(for Charlie Richardson)

If you were a truck driver
paralyzed for life by a bad road / the state had made
If you had your back smashed
Because the truck turned over
And you were six feet six two hundred fifty pounds
And the steel nailed you in and splintered your bones
because the Sec'y of State and The Commissioner of Roads
and the construction company head and the governor himself
made a deal to steal
& instead of using good concrete or quality asphalt
saved a nickel an inch and the road caved in
and faulty metal plates made the big truck flip
and it tore up your hip and put you Big Mike
in bed for life, if that was you what would you do?
If that was who? Was you. Or you. Or us. Or me.
What would we do? What would we be? And would the fire in
    our brains
ever come roaring out? I mean would we cry or shout?
What would we see except the four walls, the flat abstract glass
The landscape on Mars, staring back full of dead ash, like the
    streets
of the Paralyzed Giant. Would quietness have bloody teeth
and blank walls contract like a closing fist, would we hate
would we love anything any longer but memory, could we sing
or follow the plot of a complex tale like our own
to the red sunset and the promise of glaring tomorrows.
And if you could see for a moment the secretary of state, the
commissioner of roads, the construction company head and the
    governor

himself, would there be any words left, could you imagine
    revenge
like in Edgar Allan Poe, could you wall them in with bells on
their   hat?
idle smoke song, no place to go . . . abstract breath . . . and
    nothing to see
if it was you, if it was me, or the brother who it really is.
Can claws talk? Is death a picture? A thing, songless.
Even as the family gathers, heaping love upon him.
Is there something you can think of, more horrible than capitalism?

1993

Tracey Elvira Burwell (1962-1994)

For Tracy, Gone At Thirty Three: An Unsolicited Eulogy

We are ignorant, violent, dangerous, unemployed. Segregated, lynched, jailed, sterilized, framed, caricatured, and dismissed as humans, the reason is that we are Black, we are not humans or even citizens of They-nited States. You know—It's because we are the lowest class as a people in this land, we are niggers.

Many people, Du Bois said, have suffered as we have, in China, Europe, Latin America, but we were real estate. Chattel. Property!

And this condition is as real, in describing the lives of Black people in America to most Americans, is as true now, in actuality, as it was then. The rulers of America just created larger slave quarters today, whole cities.

They blame us for our conditions, as slaves created from the beginning up to and including this very moment, by greedy Heathens who still treat us as property—private property under slavery, public, state and government property post-slavery, and now again they seek to destroy all public democratic institutions and rule through private corporations in urban plantations and Bantustans.

Every day we have been in America our children have been murdered by the greed of the slave owners. The animalistic brutality of racist national oppression and super exploitation. They killed our children on the boats bringing us here in chains. They killed our children on the plantations. Our life expectancy as adults was seven years, 18 to 25 (this is the age group, **now**, of the one out of every four Black males, in prison or otherwise tied to the criminal criminal injustice system.) They have killed our children since we got here or torn them away from their families, to sell.

White supremacy legitimatized slavery and vice versa, just as the American courts have. The American govenment at all levels. Black people have always been suppressed by violence and fraud, "covered" by a deliberately maintained mass ignorance. So that the rich and the ignorant can tell us every day that they are mis-educating our children for our own good.

They tell us that it is our children's fault they are unemployed, because they are evil. That the schools are bad because we don't care. They tell us the violence and drugs in our communities are our fault. They speak of "Black on Black crime" or our genetical-ly, racially, caused inferiority and violence.

They make no mention that these little children with their hats turned around backward are not bringing the drugs or guns in, nor are they the ones getting rich. They tell us our children are dying because we are to blame, not a society so evil it brought us here in the bottom of slave ships (for money and because they are lazy) and holds us down in slavery, wasting our children like refuse.

They tell we parents that we have not raised our children right —that we do not care—what a hideous cynical racist lie! We care, We love and fight for our children's lives, yet they are taken from us everyday.

I knew this young woman most of her life. She grew up across the street from us, playing with our children. Her parents and grandparents tried to move the world for her. She was loved, edu-cated, trained in the arts. And she was a person of great talent as singer and dancer. Yet when she went out of her parents' home, she was attacked by the jungle of society and systematically destroyed. Like so many of our children, by the madness of the streets which is maintained by an unfair evil system created to make money for a few and exploit everybody else.

This child's mother and uncle and I and my sister grew up together in this town. This child's grandmother and grandfather were close friends of my parents, even before Jean (her mother) and I were born. Her grandmother knew me (and loves to bring it up) when I was a dangerous house-wrecking brat.

And you all and we all know how our parents and we ourselves have struggled to save our children. Yet they are abandoned by racism and greed. Even by people who look like us, who help kill our children by representing our enemies better than they repre-sent us.

And it is these same people whose job it is to blame the victims! To cover the real torturers and murderers, to tell us we threw our own selves in the bottom of the boat.

So when they come to you parents and brothers and sisters and friends of our children and tell us that they killed themselves and tell us it is our fault, scream at them that THEY LIE! Remind them of slavery and segregation and national oppression and lack of opportunity, the reasons ghettoes exist today. Tell them, Tracy was a beautiful intelligent young lady, destroyed by an uncaring evil greedy racist society.

When they blame us for surrounding our children with poverty and violence and disease, remind them that there is only one black Senator, never a black President, only a few in Congress. Tell them if we had the power (Like Marvin Gaye sang, "If This World Was Mine! . . .") If the U. S. had ever been a democracy or we had been citizens (which we have never been). If we had democracy or Self-Determination, Tracy would be alive and well and famous as an actress throughout the world. If this was "our world," (like the monster imperialism has made it "theirs") if we owned the banks and insurance companies and big corporations, Tracy and all our tragic children would be alive, just like theirs.

So scream at them that they lie! We know who controls this city, this county, this state, this country, the world and they have always hated and exploited us. Tell them we know how and why our tragic daughter here died and whose fault it really is! Scream at them **They Lie!** Then after a prayer given in Tracy's name, beautiful, lost Tracy, turn and get back to the work and struggle, help bring the unity of all the Tracys and their parents and brothers and sisters, and all the working people and oppressed nations of the world, to help save the rest of our children.

1995

Toni Cade Bambara (1939-1995)

Toni

Ah, there is a steadily more greedy shadow alienating us from our memory. That comes with time, which consumes us finally, to make us history.

The consciousness of this, we mark by the completeness of our perception, rationale and use of the world. But also by the hostility and sadness pressed upon us by death. The death of our friends. Especially of those whom we agree were, in some way, wondrous. Those who have left the brain prints of their minds and visions upon our lives and upon the world's.

Particularly, for a people deprived of the primitive normalcy of bourgeois democracy and self determination. Particularly, for a people identified by their physical appearance as slaves, those "who can be slapped," those whose torture provides the wealth, philosophical measure and social stability of a world, my grandmother said, God let be ruled by the Devil.

I know now why old people seem so removed from the tipsy gibberish of topical surfaces. They grow lonely, through the years, because the people they are closest to, the ones they have loved, laughed and reasoned with, have passed. With the absurd quickness of the years.

Witness our friend here, Toni Cade Bambara, who would make us smile when we saw her. Who would make us feel more significant in the world. Because she was one of those wondrous presences who could prove her, and all our, being, by being a living site, a conscious profile of creating.

Harlem born, Harlem Hip, Toni was always direct when you saw her, but the ironies of what she could see spread her words into a splash of narrative invocation. The quick flash of inference. She had a kind of drollery I match with the city. So she was always with us. At the front. No matter where she was. Toni was never

Blank to the world. She spoke back to it. She was engaged with it, mind and person. A woman of evocation and imagination. She was, like Jimmy or Margaret, a witness, but on her own terms. Spinning the matter with the due west breath of the new world.

Bambara, she dug out of her family's reflections. For she was with us in embracing Africa, as the place of origin of what she was, but although she called herself a nationalist and a feminist some years ago, the rush and spirit and tone of democracy, as quest, certain as love, confused as distance, was always there.

So that she felt the balance of our world. The union of our two historic selves. The African. The American. The Black and Blueness of our Am.

Last night, Amina remembered Toni, though self identifying as Black nationalist and sensitive to our culture, still was never as wild a cultural nationalist as some of us! But she was born in the Big Apple, an uptown Griot and learned from the street's memory the corniness of atavism. Toni was surprising because she would take independent looks at "Dis" and still shoot out the Bull's eye.

Toni was part of the rush of Black women writers that flowed out of the Black Arts '60s, a smoking magma of the real. Who converted the concrete dialectic of our struggle into a complex reflection of people's lives and minds.

But she was on the case. Not with a fiery pitchfork, but an insistent rationalism. She wanted to give our feelings names and addresses. So we could better understand how many and diverse are the ways and paths of revelation.

Toni knew what all the advanced know. That we are circumscribed by what we are as well as what we are not. That America has never been a democracy, and we have never been citizens!

She gave a living cast to our real life struggles. A contemporary human dimension to our dreams and our torture. She wrote of Black people, women, men, children, as workers, mothers, wives, husbands, sons and daughters, revolutionaries, militants, community organizers, nationalists, their families, the participants, the onlookers, bystanders . . . innocent or otherwise. She created a cast of the real people of our world. The selves and their consciousnesses, of where we were and wanted to go to. Our grace and our backwardness. The strength and the fragility it becomes when denied. What are the lives of conscious, progressive Black people, beset by themselves as the illness of captivity, the psychology of resistance as well as submission. She got up close on Black men and women, as a precise observer, who is a woman, advocating we get real, narrating the layers of unrealness our oppression, our ignorance, our denial, our opportunism, our momentary victory, can produce.

Her women are advanced intellectuals, as working women, activist sisters resisting Brothers insisting on locking them up in their own male delusion. Women, mostly Black, who are strong as, and mostly stronger than, their Black men. Who must convince themselves not to reveal it, even to themselves. But who must, even down to the smallest benediction. The conversational goodbye, as explanation of our movement, of Her and Him, We and Them.

But she asked, "Are you sure you want to get well?" to us all. Why was her great creativity, like all of ours, not tied by us, all together, more tightly? So many of us gone, going soon. So much pain whizzing around. More than enough!

Our bright revolutionary generation. And it's fantastic desires. Its beauty. Its strength. Its struggle. Its accomplishment. Its legacy. What will that be?!

Because, like the Bambara, we must use our highest flights of vision and creativity as the intellectual headquarters of our struggling nation. For Toni knew, so well, the truth of this oppressed Afro-American Nation. We worked together with Thulani Davis and Wesley Brown in Louis Massiah's Du Bois film. When you see it, notice how clear she is. How matter of fact about the meaning and motion of history. Listen to her. What we know, if we find a precise use for what we have already given a name.

The very removal of our friends and comrades. Large and small. All those, who like Toni, used their vision to explain the world to us, so we could change it.

Before the deadline of our lives, the experience and maturity, the moving art that Toni created, is part of the direction we must travel as a collective consciousness. Because we are in a world where even the leaders of our struggle can oppose democracy with religion and its baggage of feudalism packaged as militance. Where an intellectual activist and veteran of our struggle, a great warrior artist, can be dismissed from the struggle as a gesture of "atonement" and love. Where Angela Davis, who, a long time ago, proved her revolutionary courage, can be booed by the backward as some grim patriarchal patriotism (same word). And we, by the millions, ride the tail of our own desire, a cynical riderless horse.

We must, in the next period, begin to transform our vision and desire into living blueprints of unity and organization for self - determination, as the first necessity of democracy. Like Toni, we must create the vision, the image, but also begin to actively intervene in the politics of Black people and the advanced of the whole of the Afro-American and oppressor nation.

We must begin to create the collective organization of ourselves, the artists and intellectuals, as an act of self-determination, so that we are free to tell Toni's life and our own. And our history. One hundred of us could create a network of collective self-reliant Black Art and the necessary organization to begin to **nationalize** our greatest weapon, ourselves and the invincibility of our truth, our history and the very plan for our liberation. Our Art Our Minds. Revolutionary Art. Democratic and Beautiful. Revolutionary Art for Cultural Revolution.

The United Front for Afro-American Self-Determination, the "Man March" must become, should be consolidated only with the intervention of revolutionary Black intellectuals and artists. Like Toni Cade Bambara, we must turn our analysis and criticism into action. For the most valuable aspect of our culture is our creativity, mobilized by true self-consciousness. We are great artists, the sons and daughters of great artists. And from the conscious self organization of that art, as a method of national development, as education, employment and the expression of our lives, we can use our art to revolutionize our lives and our people's and America's. We must create a national network of artists and intellectuals, to nationalize Afro-American Culture as a total resource for Self-Determination.

Revolutionary Black intellectuals must unify and organize a national union of Afro American Artists and Intellectuals. As the creators of and catalysts for revolutionary change, upon Black people and the world. In every city or community where we are. Create. Communicate. Unite. Organize. We are given opportunity by the abuse of our enemies. Whose glitzy emptiness has long since abandoned Art, Truth and Reality for Money, Lies and Power.

Instead of whining, asking why—why can't we be all of ourselves in the world and tell our story and say how we live our lives? Then laugh at the gullible Bloods who rooted for OJ (but not Mumia). Who have no question for the Minister, or the others who admire foolish Negroes and cruel whip crackers. The cultural canon of national oppression, its philosophy, influence, psychology and stolen wealth, must be neutralized and prevented from stealing more of our soul's wealth, and misdirect, condemn and doom our people.

In every city, there is a Motown! A collective of the city's history and heartbeat. We must provide an economic base for ourselves, collectively and take intellectual responsibility for our people's level of development, not by cynicism and alienation or being a drowned fly in the sour buttermilk of "white america," the oppressor nation.

Stop bowing to our enemy! Communicate! Organize! Produce! Unify the Afro-American political culture with the development of a national Black Artists and Intellectuals Network, for self-determination, self-consciousness, self-reliance and self-defense. Use the art to provide resources, education, employment and political unity. We can fight in the superstructure. The class struggle in the realm of ideas.

Let us begin, before we lose another wonderful friend. "We have a better future than that," Toni said. That's what Toni was saying. Be Clear. Understand. Act! Make the Revolution!

*   *   *

(At the National Black Arts Festival in 1994, Toni, Amina, Wesley Brown, Michael Simmons and I sat up most of the night in the lobby of the Mariott kicking these ideas around, as we have done before. Then we started singing. We went from the sorrow songs become Freedom songs, and then for the last couple hours, Toni and Wesley and Amina started singing Oldies But Goodies, into the Gems of American Popular Song. Toni played piano and sang and She and Wesley wailed. Man, was that hip!

I should ask Toni, now, if she remembers. Toni is saying, "Make the Revolution!")

1995

Tina Johnson-Landrum (1930-1995)

Takalifu

Tina was an old friend of ours. A friend based not on casual or superficial things. Tina. Takalifu was actually what you'd call a Sister in struggle. Tina was part of an objective united front against Black national oppression and for democracy and self-determination that had been given leadership and even some organizational dimension by the Committee for Unified Newark and then by the Congress of African People, after CFUN led the mobilization of the masses in the late '60s that finally resulted in the election of Newark's 1st Black mayor, Kenneth Gibson.

Tina was part of that upsurge, the many of us, who in struggle, came into a fuller consciousness, not only of ourselves, but of the world which we now would swear to change. But changing the world, even some small part of it, is hard work. There are easy solutions. God might rule in Heaven, but the Devil definitely rules this planet.

But in the late '60s and early '70s we were still young and we thought, a lot of us, that we could whip the devil in a few minutes, certainly now that we had determined to do that and even focused on it, what we could understand was evil. Because that's all the devil is, the one that is doing d/evil.

We did not understand completely, then, the whole nature of the struggle, with our energy and fire. For one thing, we did not understand the protracted nature of the struggle. That it would be a long haul, a distance race, not a sprint, that it would take deep resolve, and growing ideological clarity, to Keep on Pushin, like Curtis Mayfield was telling us.

So through the years, Tina, Takalifu was her Swahili name, had worked together w/ us many many times on many projects. Tina was one of those community people who the struggle brings forward and helps educate. Because there is nothing that educates us deeper and quicker than revolutionary struggle. What it would take you years to learn normally, you might learn in a few days. That is the nature of struggles for social transformation.

This is a constant note of sadness sounded because so many of us are getting out of here. So many of our old friends. This is sharpened by the thought that all of us, when we met, and I see many of you in the congregation . . . old movement veterans . . . when we met, we thought by this time things would be totally different, totally changed. You know this is not the case. If anything, many aspects of our lives are worse now than they were 25 years ago. Even many of those things that we might have thought were better, if we look into closely, we might be sadly surprised.

One aspect of our struggle that I associate with Takalifu is the one around education. In fact, isn't it deeply ironic that just a few days after the slave master and her overseers overrun our city and take over the Newark Board of Education, our sister leaves us! I guess she just couldn't stand to see that happen. Because Tina was with us, my wife, Amina and the others, when we began fighting for an elected school board. Yes, it was the people themselves who fought and won an elected board. We understood that was the most democratic way to involve the community in the education of their own children. And so we worked, Tina among us, to get the elected school board. And we were elated when it came into being, because we thought we could really step forward then. Amina and I had seven children in the Newark school system. Takalifu was a Newark school mother too.

How sad now to understand that that long struggle was just one more struggle in the war for democracy and self determination. Because for Black people, America has **never been** a democracy. And Black people have **never been citizens**. They try to prove that to us every day. Whether it's a little California Hitler, like Pete Wilson, leading the destruction of affirmative action at the University of California, or the right wing New Jersey governor, Whitman, suppressing our vote to get elected, backing the Rutgers president, Lawrence, who thinks we are "genetically inferior" or when she talks about "Jewels in the Crown," to explain unwed mothers, when she and her bougeois friends got both the jewels and the crown. Or now sending state troopers in to take over the Newark schools; so they can steal the education budget and give tax breaks to the suburbanites and cash and new "markets" from privatization, and so run the city from the statehouse—just like a plantation.

In order to live like they do, they have to have their money and ours. In order for them to keep us living like we do, they must keep robbing us, and keep us uneducated. Call us out our names. And then like the storm trooper slave masters we know them to be, come rushing into Newark talking about they are going to educate our children.

Tina knew that was a lie. She was with us so many times going to Trenton to protest the slave legacy school system that our being slaves and then discriminated against and segregated had brought. So, like many others, it seemed the height of evil for the slave-master, who had thrown you to the bottom of human social life, with his laziness and love of idleness, to then tell you that you are suffering the effects of his murderous "humanity." And blame you! Kidnap you from your home, enslave you 500 years, doing the work to make them rich, then call you LAZY!

Tina ran for the school board on the ticket we put together in the '80s, SAVE THE CHILDREN. It was a good campaign, but we didn't win. Partially, because some of the same people who opposed the elected school initially now saw a way to get rich off it. Some of these same Negroes who sit back and say nothing, now the slave masters have figured it's time for their counter-attack.

This would make Tina's eyes grow into tight little dangerous bb's when we would discuss not only the outright enemies, but those Negroes who we had entrusted with our lives and who, it is very clear now, have failed to do anything except stuff their pockets, (usually with "chump change").

I gave a eulogy for Joseph Smiley Landrum, her husband, who for so long supported Tina in her will to struggle. Tina went ahead and got her an education, even while raising her children and still taking part in the people's struggle to change the world. She was Chairman of the *People's Democratic Council*, which was formed as a people's city council, to take up those tasks the other city council would not. Actually, as a way of arousing the people so they would fight against our oppression and exploitation in a more consistent and informed way.

Takalifu was small, round and laughing. That's how we remember her. A roly poly, happy engine of movement and work. She was part of the struggle and this is the legacy she leaves her family and the rest of us. One of the millions of barely known activists, the backbone of our struggle. And we see now that struggle must yet continue, that we are visited by the demoniacal Sisyphus syndrome once again. Where we, Black Sisyphus, roll the rock of struggle for self determination and democracy up to the top of the mountain, only to have evil "Gods" roll it back down on our heads, again.

These middle '90s we are at the bottom of the mountain once again, and many of our staunchest fighters have now gone on. But if we think about what they were fighting for, like Tina, if we remember how dedicated and sincere and good she was, it should give us a deeper resolve, as if she passed on all that strength and love and commitment to us. That is as it should be. I know that's what Takalifu would want.

1995

William Kunstler (1919-1995)

Bill the Kunstler

What about the fact that all of these Eulogies are for Black people excpet his one and Mikey Piñero's?? It dont have to be elaborated on, it speaks for itself. And, like my man, very eloquently so. And he supposedly had the law on his side (though not the courts).

Bill was a brother I knew because of my own activities, pro-clivities and commitment and I knew him, naturally enough, because of his. There's very few people in the Black Liberation Movement or the general anti-imperialist and with that, radical or progressive or people's democratic struggle against U. S. imperial-ism, racism, women's oppression, anti-democracy, worker's exploitation, who wouldn't know Bill Kunstler. (His last name is German for Artist . . . and he certainly was, ask the minions he fought for, the poor, the workers, Blacks, Latinos, the oppressed nationalities, the homeless, women, and on).

Bill was, like they say, a standup guy. But he stood up against the Great Behemoth of UGLY, mainly the U.S. Govt, its corrupt and racist judicial system, it's undemocratic courts, and its Amer-ican-as-Apple-Pie-Gestapo police, FBI, CIA & DEA. Look at the major cases of struggle in this country against national oppres-sion, big capital, for civil rights of all descriptions, in the last 40 or so years and sure enough you'll find bad Bill right in the mid-dle of them.

He even had a couple cases of mine. One he got me off, the oth-er was tossed out. You felt comfortable with Bill out there doin it for you. His manner in the court was altogether Bill. He walked into these courts, like he actually knew who or rather what, was presiding and why. Many lawyers don't even know that . . . .I don't mean the judge's name, but who he (or she) is working for, ultimately, a repressive bourgeois state.

And Bill began all his cases with this knowledge and this stance. He had an answer for almost anything the Judges might throw up or the usually asinine prosecutors. He was especially fine tripping up lying police. And this always earned him the smirking contempt of the judge, or sometimes straight out contempt citations. Check how many times Bill did time because he faced some nasty (sometimes nazi) Judge with the truth. Or because he exposed the system itself, for what it is, a society run by the rich to keep them that way and richer, which then, of necessity, must exploit and repress working people.

What impressed me most deeply, or more precisely, educated me about Bill Kunstler was the clear example of class stance being most important in the struggle against international villainy, not nationality or gender or sexual orientation, etc. (Or whatever else the bourgeoisie comes up with to muddy and confuse the struggling people.) Certainly these are all struggles for democracy, which gives them a commonality, but too often the leading forces (not necessarily, unfortunately, the advanced forces) are so small—grouped off according to nationality, gender, sexual orientation, etc.—that the Big Dog can get over with his time worn, but still reliable, Big Caesar gambit, divide and conquer.

Because even in the church of narrow nationalism or bourgeois feminism or sectarian gayness, there were always folks reaching out for Bill Kunstler. That was a given in the movement, in any serious aspect of its total expression. If you got jammed by Uncle Jam or any of his United Snakes, the cry would go up, "Get Bill Kunstler." (But I guess that same cry went up many times among the Dogs of War themselves, with different meaning.)

From the civil rights struggles across the South against the most American of Nazis, with King and SCLC, with Stokely and Rap and SNCC, with Bobby and the Panthers in the infamous New Haven frame up. In the Chicago proto-Hitlerian so called "Chicago Seven" case, which followed the "Days of Rage," where a certain Judge Hoffman actually gagged Panther leader, Bobby Seale, just to show the world that Bloods were still 3/5ths of a swine, and if you tried to put your "two cents" in, you would get, literally, gagged.

Consider just a few of the huge cases in which this radical Kunstler, as the people' warriors, was on the frontline defending Martin Luther King, Adam Clayton Powell, Stokely Carmichael, Bobby Seale, Daniel Berrigan, The Attica Brothers. (Remember, also, Bill trying to negotiate with Rocky and his assassins!)

It was Kunstler, as well, who defended Wayne Williams in the Atlanta Child Murders, and although Williams went to jail, implicitly put on the spot for all the murders, Bill had proof that the Klan was involved, just as he had come up with the proof, years before, that two of the three men imprisoned for the Malcolm assassination were framed. But, of course, the courts successfully muffled all this, as they always do to protect the renegade state.

And most recently, that slam dunk he did against the Feds in their pitiful attempt to frame Malcolm X's daughter for mistakenly believing Minister Farrakhan had something to do with her father's murder. (And they, of all people, certainly knew the error of this view, since they killed Malcolm themselves.) Bill was usually right "on it" and his contributions to the struggle for democracy should never be diminished. He was always on the scene and ready to rumble.

Bill Kunstler was also a man of principle. I remember he called me to be a character witness for an up-and-coming Newark boxer, who at the time was fairly well known, at least by boxing fans. He was in the slam for murder. I met Bill in the courthouse and was ready to go in and testify, when as he was briefing me about the case, I discovered that this guy did pull this murder, in fact it was one of my cousins he had killed. One with the same first name as I was given, Everett.

Naturally, I nixed that. But then Bill nixed it right after that. He had been fighting to get this brother out because he believed that, like so many of the one out of four Black males in jail or in some other way held fast in the U.S. web of Black national oppression, that the dude was probably innocent in the first place, as so many are. But when he got the word that, no, this was the actual dude, then Bill "booked" very shortly thereafter.

Bill Kunstler proved to me for many years the possibility of multinational struggle for democracy and socialism in the U.S.

Because it is finally in our practice, our acts, that our revolutionary commitment is shown. It is our concrete participation in the anti-imperialist, anti-racist struggle, that will unify us, regardless of the other concomitant aspects which still sadly separate so many of the oppressed, repressed, and exploited from each other. It is this always-raging struggle for democracy that is the "fuel" for the masses of people's moves to fully revolutionary positions.

But Bill was, like too many of us, overworked, stressed out past the moon, and constantly confronting the cruel, the ignorant & the greedy, which, brothers and sisters, let me assure you, can take a whole lot out of you.

Remember, while we are demonstrating, or writing tracts or essays, or circulating petitions, or marching, or like Bill, preparing our briefs, staying up night after night to get fully prepared for yet another skirmish with the actual unmetaphysical devil, Devil and co. are laid back somewhere, maybe Bermuda, grooving on our children's flesh.

Bill Kunstler was a Law Artist, but he was also a soldier, like the brother told me who called to inform me of this blow to people struggling for democracy all over the world. I got this call and the brother, Akita, who had once been defended by Bill as well, said simply, "One of our soldiers has died." Yeh, that about sums it up, I'd say.

Except, for those who didn't know Bill, or at least who he was, or his work, there was, like us all, another side of him. He was, literally, an artist. He wrote sonnets for Bill Tatum's *Amsterdam News* every week. Many of them were at least, hilarious and cutting, but Bill's real art was the law. The court-room was his gallery, where his work was shown. His patrons were revolutionaries, the suffering people. His critics were, well you know who most critics work for, Richie Death.

The last time I saw Bill, it was with my wife, Amina, at his birthday party down in the village, right around the corner from where he lived for years. Naturally, Bill Tatum was there, but one thing I remember, aside from the many activists, like Big Black and others from the infamous Attica case (where Governor Rockefeller ordered the police to kill 40 inmates and they killed correction officers as well. Then tried to blame the murder of the correction officers on the inmates, issuing a report that they had all died with their throats cut. And then, when it was investigated, it was revealed that the guards, the state's employees, had been murdered by the state gunmen as well! Let that be a lesson to some of you slow types!)

I remember arguing all night with some famous mad comedian, who was a long-time friend of Bill's. (But hadn't it been obvious that even if I didn't agree with this dude (we were arguing about O. J.) that it was obvious that he was on the left. And that as I looked around I could see a lot of people I knew, many I didn't, who were also some kind of radicals or progressives, hey, even a few of my paisans, communists. I got a warm rush out of that, all these folks had come to pay homage to The Law Artist, the Soldier, the revolutionary democratic warrior. And it made me feel real good. That I knew such a man. And that he, like some of us, had never shrunk from his responsibilities, his war gig, over the long haul, the protracted struggle that this overthrow of imperialism will take. There he was, in full view, laughing, and arguing (naturally), but he had taken a minute to check out my own teapot struggle and he chuckled and winked.

I felt warmed, actually somewhat refreshed and giving Bill the shrug of "Yeh, I know," I returned to my own skirmish and thought aint it hip that we can hold maneuvers for our more serious confrontation with the U. Snakes and still be amongst serious minds and having a good time with Bill The Law Kunstler.

Everyone who understands the world and wants to change it, would miss Bill, especially in these sad times of reaction and rising fascism. For me, it's like an insurgent on the battlefield who's just been told one of his most effective weapons is missing.

I know the next time I see him he'll be fighting these same forces, whatever they call themselves where he is.

1995

Don Gabriel Pullen (1941-1995)

Don Pullen Leaves Us

Don, you too, already? So many of us away away. We were here
& sang and spoke and danced and played and even made war.
Acted. We did—

And from that time I first met you and Milford, your man.
That home-made self-made intro side. I donno, people kept saying
this and that, you was more or less than this or that one. It didn't
and don't matter. You was hip as Don Pullen and very few can
claim that.

So sad, brother, very few of the citizens even know yr name.
Very few even got to know you—your music. Very few.

Don, so beautiful, yet still in my mind, a young man. Don,
Don, so beautiful. Yet like my whole gang of great genius moth-
erfuckers, so quickly gone. Don, so beautiful. Still. I see you, still
so young. With so much fire and incredible vision, loveliness blue
gleaming funk pouring out of your fingers. Don. Don, so beautiful. I see you, still a very young man, and yet so quickly, like so
many of our gang, already gone. No glibness. It just aint hip
enough here. It is the ugliness and terror surrounding this little
light of ours.

We wanted in and wanted out! We needed, like that song, and
you did appear and grow and gave the gift the Dr. spoke of. The
gift of song and story, and yes, the gift of labor, and the gift of
spirit. These are the gifts of Black Folk, the visible daylight fire
that alone keeps us alive, prevents our death by frostbitten heart-
lessness, the maniac heathen who own this space, bloodily maintain and claim, no shit, that it's civilization.

Yet with these gifts of ours, the gifts of Black Folks, just this
week, you, Julius Hemphill and Gil Moses, all here, less than six
decades, have gone, been swept away—By what? And that's the
question plagues me, that what that why and lack of wise.

Swept away by Dis. And Covered. Even while living. From lost Columbus, given the word by Isabella (a lie), that the Moors was whipped. El Sid had triumphed (and was getting a radio gig at Birdland) and that it was cool to hotfoot to "India" to pick up some taste for the grit. But they meant a dimension, a thing, for their newstyle "Christianity" of pretense.

So the D at the end of Go. De fense against Go. Against life. The D. The Thing of Heathen fusion lie with death. The Idol. For life is eating and drinking and farting and belching and rape (the F word) and rape their last name.

And then to give it Greatness. Here. Everywhere. They cd not lead, but give it the same timbre as Dead. Without life. If we were Shines. They cd get Shiny The God—Better The Thing The Stopping of Life. GOLD.

Space becomes Speech becomes money. The Sun's very rays are said to be in competition with other. As they race across the not see, these blind heathens saw Races, of everyone. In order to belch and fart more. The most deadly animal can pretend.

And here we come, the Afro'mericans. The source of the riches. Af—Before, but seized by Romans. Roaming ourselves, dragged here to the money lovers' (Ame ricans) stolen palace. Our chants at night under the decks. Our screams to whatever it was we'd forgotten. Because we seized ourselves and gave ourselves to Rome, we were so high. And that's how we got down.

When I met you, like me. We knew we would win the world. We knew it didn't belong to no Heathens. That's why you wailed so hard uptown with us. We Black Arts them nights Cooking us black Harlem magic.

We owned Black Art! We cried We Black. We coming Out. All in The Street. We cried was revolutionaries. That our hearts beat tempos. Our language itself was syncopation. And Blue we painted on us from the inside. So our spirits were dark like our mother night.

So Don was out! All of us was Out. Trying to get out. Already Out! Going Out further. Trane was our underground railroad. Albert Ayler was the high whistle you heard that broke the nights into dances the stars sparkling notes the sky played.

You see we thought Art was Tatum, Blakeley, at least Farmer, that it was the prayer the dark folks whispered "And Thou Art with me." Our Art was our comrade in struggle. It was the creation creating that wished us here. Ain't's enemy. We played the Blues from our memory. When we were Home. And so came again to Harlem to try to get back.

We knew what then we had to do to make us so Black & Blue. The out was to be counted. Along with Count & Duke & Billie & Bud & Monk & Bird & Pres. The Out was to escape—this jail of colorless evil. We were our own spices.

(Besides we knew Columbus was a torturer and a criminal and he brought spies to seize our goods and make everything else bad [in english] And call himself God. Removing the second circle of infinity the Art would turn upside down like a smile becomes a frown [womens got sad] and vision would become a broke carrier an unmoving cart to carry something that does not exist. Tragedy's taxi. [You know. God riding a machine!])

If G is the Sun Gone from Nut the speech of the balls track through space like the earthy clitoris touching itself and becoming the Ark. the SDG. The coming. The Sea man. In waves. Ultra purple invisible to the circle of lo! To the second circle of go! To the third circle of soul created and gone. Then what created is good. What Is created. And it is alive. Not a statue or a statute (a paper statue) A low opposite. It is the truth. The they is it going. The ing in we connected to coming. The jism is the jasm. It says I AM. JAZZ. Signed with Shango's initials. I AM. We say through eternity. Speaking from the sky. SHA-N-GO! ZZ JA (Yes! Eye! I! Aye!) AM. We could feel that we were invoking that goodness and truth and beauty was swinging. That like come it was hot. We were the Out of Ja who cd C. We were Ja's coflation. A little food from thought. The arc was Blue. Our memory too. And we were like every thing forever. Black. But when we studied and worked and fought we had read the book of life. And our outness exploded Red. We knew we were new. So we blew what we knew. What we blew, that made us blue. And we read every body.

We wanted to Change Everything. The Changes we went through we saved like Black mama becoming the 1st Say lore.

Our needs were Know I see. The So—The Sown. The Changes were sewn in us. And we spread them like the seeds of our thoughtfulness.

Like the nigger of eternity we loved freedom. We could see it when we got in to the Visionary thought, the question that beats Are I Them! The answer the down of the turning waves, possessed by their going and coming, the rise and falls, and the curves of the five senses, the black notes of Human Number, the symbol of Self—connected to the circle of going, Knowing, a speed measured in knots, the body of our rise the swift swoop. And funk of our fall. Getting down is the motion and Time and Art. Like Sisyphus rumbling to the bottom of the mountain—again.

We knew we had to go on out to get past the dead and the executioner's symbol they bid us wear to show we loved the prophet's murder. They said they would give us candy, to show how the dead could rise again a few days later. And the prophet's betrayal would be our namesake, the graves to trick us with Sweet History Month, they covered with chocolate. That world, the moon, matter, the motion, became Peter-Paul's Mounds.

We would play the new world. Not be hung by our balls like the old father who denied us or the self-hating convert who covered us on the Road to Rome, who never was an apostle. Peter and Paul were the creators of Rock and Roll.

We were new souls, children WHO. M. B. The WE of US & I. Albert, Pharoah, Sun Ra. We all was on the same Trane. With Henry Dumas and Larry Neal, out's children. An army of RAZORS. An army of Bloods. (Check *Richard's Tune* and *Big Alice*).

We seemed Strange because we were the change. Don was telling us Jesus never been in Europe! He was telling us Everybody talking Bout Heaven Aint Going There. Listen to *Malcolm and Betty*. He was telling us The Ballot or The Bullet.

Don wd play the black notes as vowels. Five of them. And the 21 consonants, a sea of trouble. Don was explaining why Ali Baba, on reaching Europe, ate fish on Friday. To eat up the old religion. He knew why the imposters called Christ's day of execution "Good Friday." And that Friday was a day of freedom for the

Heathens, since they had killed the Son and taken Summer north and named him Remus.

He knew how the Sun Man's lost child was kidnapped to the out lands. And the opposite side of the whirl was called Romulus. How the brothers Romulus and Remus were Sumer and Sulumoor. And how Bird swept up through the nut of his black mama, black rising against blue bursting into flames at the top. Celebrating himself and everything that Are.

He was our Eye. That Black Fetish Djeli Ya Bird. Inside his mother watching the wolf, where the flood waters swept, suckle them and whisper about Johannesburg.

Don knew Gold was a Dead Thing. That money was a blind liar chanting that Heaven was a plantation full of slaves. Don spoke in a swirl of pictures. Like the voice of our mother the sky, when she is wet and on fire. Only truth is royal. Only reality.

His self was a thought of laughter. The smile from the bottom of the world. He was the Who that ends as Be. Though at the footstep of down rush spirit, invisible breathing. Don could get high from smiling. He rode the blue ark of flight. He was U and U The I & I of Birth and Vision. He cd sweep across the keys like educated space speaking in colors.

He used sound as the spectrum of particularity. Like the notes were things with lives and business. He was warm and alive yet he would scream and hammer like Shango's boy telling everybody where he was.

He was the romance. The living ocean of human life. Don was communicating what civilization is. He was a spirit (reliverer). He'd leave you with a spirit embracing you. He turned you Blue. He forced you to act like you read the world every day. He made you fly and see from up there how small how awe full, yet like the numberless flowers, funky pretty smelling and beautiful waving to the birth nap, the horns and bass.

Don loved Love. He wanted, like, all of us living humans, to be love, to make everything love and the truth. Don wanted everything to swing like it should. To whisper and scream and kiss and embrace themselves as other everybodies cool as the chorus of comets.

Don. I cant love you enough for you to be here now playing. Yet we will someday save ourselves by forgetting this animal world. Letting them go to Mars in a Hot Rush. While we float on the blue water the see of the whole self. The mother of the father, the son of the all's daughter. The vision the fission the colored say lores the tale oars of the wordship. The go past, this world, must change, even while we sit here or blow the devil, backward life, away.

I want to hear Don inside me like that beyond the space of time the lies of how wise got to be spelled w-h-i-t-e.

We are The Razor. Don wd play, We are The Blood. He was new, like we all were. He came from Out to bring those hundred flowers of his fingers, to return those hundred schools of spiritual fish, back home. Don was a point guard of the new, the yet, the will, the beauty of humanity still emerging. Don was post-Heathenic loveliness. Post imperialist musart. Eye him later Who 1st was the me you cant see.

We were there, the answer electricity gives to the be seer. Beau Peep! Hot eye the blue spook, afraid of a thing who says it lives and is dead, the backward dog. The lead foot of the lame who left home a murderer who went north to be a mf and get blind and eat people. Later he started calling it religion, the prize for bribing judges, the cost of becoming Holy **and** the Vampire. Yet still **We** color the world. Co Author it with the birth of each you reliving.

Don was not known widely because he was a tour few take. So he rode the ark in the asking cycle. And hammered like old speech the keys to open tomorrow.

We got high possessed and rose blue like flying, to escape these animals before. Up this tree of life and made hands of our feet and thumbs of our toes. The apples the naked liars copped (the adman and the imaginary woman he created for their pet serpent) were actually solid waste. And for the predators this was money. Yet they were insulted by our high ness. They did not understand we were possessed by what rises into where, not a sum, but an every, each return, on the ladder, like up in the tree you cd hear them crying, limping there hairy with a club. And cdn't clam up no how.

My eyes were rolling like the universe. Don speaking. There is

no place but what I make travels and loves and is the family looking up at the Sun.

Don was my brother. He could sing to me like from a very old
place, and I would feel and hear and understand. And then we
would be flying. Black up rising against the guinea blue. In my
memory. Don is the future waiting to say hello again. And we
know life does not end. Don, if you dig it, is where ever Blue is,
still goin out, playing himself, in that moving arc of light, he cir-
cles just above our heads, invisible and nuclear, telling quiet stories in the voice of the mother tongue, so we are never alone.

1995

Russell Bingham

Baba

My earliest memory of Baba Mshauri (Father Advisor), what some other folks later call Consigliere, was when I was a young boy, not even teenage. He was one of the shining Players who moved in that glitter of first awakening in a golden place called the Grand Hotel. Really. Some of you old folks know it well. When Newark still had a Black entertainment and business district, before the Dis called integration. When we had a Black baseball team, the Newark Eagles. They were the last world champions (of the Negro National League) of that bygone "seemingly" happy age.

And the Grand Hotel, on West Market Street, was where they cavorted. My father, used to take me there after the Eagles had whooped up on somebody. I met Monte Irvin and Larry Doby and Pat Paterson and Leon Day, who pitched a no-hitter opening day that last year. They were the grand heroes of my age. A Black woman, Effa Manley, a friend of my parents, owned that team.

And in that surrounding, that millieu of light and fantasy, correspondance with all of our higher selves, I was also introduced to Russell Bingham. A Player, like they say. And you could tell it. Even I could, at my young age, I knew this was somebody different. He was always, every day I spotted him in my life, absolutely impeccable, clean as a new day and cool, as we old folks say, like an icy flame. But that's what the blues is.

He shook my hand, along with other giants of that time. That was where, it seemed to me, the highlight of life was to be lived, in that Grand Hotel, West Market Street, Newark. Light conversation and intense laughter, good feelings and an organist named Pitts, stroking in the backup to keep it all moving, blue and thoughtful.

Then some twenty years later, just down the corner really, at

502 High Street, around 1968, we met again. This time about some adult matters. I had finally made it. We were part of a group called the United Brothers, who determined to share, once a week, all the stripes of political information and consolidate them. All the diverse ideological stripes we wanted to bring together, to concentrate on what we needed to deal with, Black Power. Malcolm ha sounded it, Carmichael had coined the term, and here in Newark we got down to the ready or not and Russell was there with us.

When the organization got more African oriented, as we became African Nationalists, some of the older folks backed up, they weren't ready for no Africa. And Russell Bingham "discovered" it too. And we named him Baba, Baba Mshauri, Father Advisor. We became The Committee for a Unified Newark, combining in the fundamental United Front form to bring all the progressive forces in the city of Newark together to end the apartheid city government structure.

Later, we'd form a national organization, The Congress of African People, of which CFN was the political center.

CAP was the successor to the old Black Power Conferences, first called by Adam Clayton Powell. The founding conference for CAP was Summer 1970 in Atlanta, right after our victory in the Kenneth Gibson election. (The same weekend the Black Panther party held their Constitutional Conference in D.C.!)

And Baba was there, a key figure in our Siasa (Politics) unit. It was Baba who really masterminded our move through electoral politics in '68-'70 and the successful election of Gibson, as the first "Black" mayor of a major northeastern city. We'd a been better with Baba as mayor! He knew politics cold, upside down, Blood Urban style. As swift and clean as his "old" self.

One day during that hotly contested struggle, the Simbas (our military arm) came flying into the Hekalu (swahili for Temple) and told me Baba and a brother named Mkuu had just caught some deputy sheriff pulling down our "Community's Choice" posters. He had a gun, this deputy, but Baba intimidated the dude, gun and all and Mkuu popped him on the glass jaw.

He was fearless, my "Consigliare". He would go up against

anyone. State. Police. City. Racists. Ignorant Negroes. Hey, they were just pests to my Baba.

When our first Negro Mayor proved to be just that, a first Negro, Baba even told me how that should'a been dealt with. Cause he could see it in my face. But, at the same time, he cautioned that it was a fool's move because we were on all the ugly peoples' laundry list.

Baba wanted to be a part of every community struggle. He was truly what you called a "Race Man"! A Black patriot! And though he was first famous in Newark for being a digital personality, like Bumpy Johnson in Harlem, a friend of his, Baba instructed me as to how Bumpy J and many of those other brothers and sisters in the numbers game had been patriots. (And after all that jail time, Bumpy, 23 years in prison, 13 in Alcatraz, now it come on every night on television "Pick Six!" Just like Elvis Presley!). It was Baba who first pointed out to me that not only the Harlem Renaissance was supported by the Digit folks, but Garvey, Adam Powell, Malcolm X and even some well known Black film stars, were a few of Bumpy and the older number people's "God children"!

And even after the organization split with ideological struggle, some to the Right, some to the Left, I still would sit and talk to Baba from time to time about his favorite subjects, Politics and the sellout Negroes downtown who had betrayed us.

But I still remember Baba, dressed as we all were then, smart in our Mwalimu Nyerere inspired National dress suits and the fist quick against the chest, our salute. We were all tuned hard and sharp, but full of the rhythm of birth and rebirth.

He told you exactly like it was. The funniest class in politics I ever had was to sit between Baba and Honey Ward, his long time buddy. Back and forth, up and down. But I was taking it all in. Baba taught most of the standup Black politicians in Newark.

Slowly, they are all leaving us. Our past, our present. The older we get, the lonelier...

What was it in Baba, that Black Fire, that always raged? As sweet as he was, you rather run through Hell with gasoline drawers, like we used to say when I was a kid, than mess with Baba.

Not just intelligence and courage, dignity, integrity. My oldest and wisest adviser.

But this is a relay race. Baba gave me that, he passed that baton to me and a lot of others. Just as I hope I am doing. Our bond was Love of Our People, courage and intelligence. As Stokely used to say, "An undying love for our people!"

Where did he come from? Ourselves!
Where has he gone? To get help!
Will he be forgotten?
                    in this age of Retrograde
                              Buppies
                                   & sell out nigger heroes?
Only if we all die, every nigger on the planet
                    then Baba will die too
                              But not until then!

                    Tutaonana, Baba!
                    Hofi Ni Kwenu!

NOTES

[Texts in italics by Amiri Baraka, notes compiled by Michael Schwartz]

John Alexander (1919-1990)

From the memorial program, Bethany Baptist Church, Newark, N.J.:

John Wesley Alexander was born in Nashville, Tennessee to Dr. Royal C. Alexander and Esther Tildon Alexander . . . He received his medical training at Meharry Medical College, Nashville, Tennessee and graduated in 1943 . . . In 1958, John was certified by the American Board of Pediatrics, and from 1958 until his passing, he demonstrated his selfless commitment to the health and welfare of the community's children. After a fire in the mid-'60s destroyed his office on Main Street in Orange, the focus of his practice shifted to Newark. His dedication to the greater Newark population mandated he maintain his presence in the inner city, rather than in the more affluent suburban areas . . .

Jimmy Anderson (1932-1992)

Jimmy was a great tenor saxophone player. He played in some of my musical projects. He wrote a book on teaching music that the Newark Board of Education, in their foolishness, rejected. In the main, he confined his career to Newark. To me, he was the kind of person who, given any kind of real opportunity or alternative to his life, could have been a very well-known musician had he been given the opportunity to do that.

James Arthur Baldwin (1924-1987)

Writing a eulogy of someone you knew in a personal way can be very strange when you are also eulogizing their cultural contributions which affected you as well. I always felt gratified to be in Jimmy's company. I was like a kid. I was finding out stuff. I had admired him from the first time I saw his face on the cover of Notes of a Native Son, *when I was coming out of the Air Force. For me, he's always been a kind of measure and a guide. At one time we had a falling out. Early in the Civil Rights Movement, he had a view that the struggle against racism that was going on could be transcended by Love. I wasn't buying any of that, and took issue with him personally for what I saw as his ignoring the struggle. I wrote this terrible review of a book of his in which, in craziness, I took this out on him. But Jimmy changed with the years. He got with Dr. King. In fact, along with King and Malcolm, one of the best known voices in the Civil Rights Movement has become James Baldwin's.*

When I was asked to eulogize him and take part in the memorial at the Cathedral of St. John the Divine in Manhattan, there was a powerful personal symbolism in this for me. I took being asked, to be almost an **assignment***, to carry on his mission. Maya Angelou, Toni Morrison and myself: it was as if we were being told You are the ones who have to carry this on. I've always taken it like that.*

Toni Cade Bambara (1939-1995)

Toni Cade Bambara's fiction illuminates and dramatizes social issues in the African-American community by exploring interpersonal relationships. In stories written between 1959 and 1970, published in her collection *Gorilla, My Love* (1972), she wrote about young children and adolescents learning to make their own ways in their neighborhoods. Between 1972 and 1977, when she published her second short story collection, *The Sea Birds Are Still Alive*, her political awareness and her esteem for women's organizations and the political value of creative community and culture were deepened by a meeting with the Federation of Cuban Women in 1973 and a trip to Vietnam in 1975 during which she met with members of the Women's Union. From 1986 until near the end of her life, she taught scriptwriting at the Scribe Video Center in Philadelphia, where she helped support the careers of emerging black women filmmakers. During this time, she worked on the production of several television documentaries, including *The Bombing of Osage Avenue*, about the police assault on MOVE headquarters in Philadelphia, and a documentary about the life of W.E.B. Du Bois.

I got to know her well when we were working on the W.E.B. Du Bois documentary. She died two days before it was shown. I appreciated her as a dynamic personality but have a profound respect for her independent and advanced view of the interrelationship of the local-personal and international-political that she had come up with on her own. Her fiction gave a human face and voice to the people who were trying to make revolution and were interested in black power and black self-determination in the '60s.

Kimako Baraka (1936-1984)

Kimako Baraka was killed January 31, 1984. She was murdered by a mentally disturbed man who she had tried to help.

I think of her often. I only had one sister. You never realize how much that means to you.

Tracey Elvira Burwell (1962-1994)

Tracy is the daughter of someone I grew up with. Her grandmother and grandfather knew my parents. The family still lives directly across the street from us now. When I was a teenager her mother and I sang in the same choirs and glee clubs. We were both products of that part of the black middle class that emphasized discipline and art-sy activities for children, to give them something and to keep them out of trouble. My sister ended up as a Broadway dancer. I took piano lessons, drumming lessons, and drawing lessons. Now that I look back, I see how this actually taught me a lot of what I know about what it takes to create something. My sister and I were both in the arts and education. It wasn't by chance; it was because our mother designed it that way. Tracy was somebody who should have gone on to become a performer and succeeded, but she got taken by the street thing. That's always such a grim and terrible possibility when you grow up in these ghettoes, even though there's a lot of middle class attempts to provide you with safe passage, that danger is out there.

From the memorial service program, Messiah Baptist Church, East Orange, N.J.:

She attended Pope Pius High School in Passaic, New Jersey and also attended the New York Academy of Acting; the Kay and Pat Thompson School of Dance; the New Jersey School of the Performing Arts; Belle Meade Modeling and Charm School; and the Alvin Ailey Dance Theater of Harlem . . . Tracey truly lived and loved life and everyone she touched. Her personality and winning smile were very contagious. We will miss her, but we are happy because we visualize no hills, no rough roads or barriers, just streets of purest gold. On this journey she will never sigh, never moan, and never get tired, because she is walking with her Saviour.

Amilcar Cabral (1924-1973)

Cabral was one of the intellectual and political leaders of the Pan-African liberation movement. As founder of the PAIGC (African Party for the Independence of Guinea-Bissau and the Cape Verde Islands) he led successful independence struggles in both of these former Portuguese colonies. Cabral was one of an elite handful of Africans who were selected to be educated in Portugal to be groomed as colonial administrators. He was trained as an agronomist but also made a systematic study of Marxism and became a Marxist theoretician who adapted classical theories to the realities of Third World economies. He put forth uniquely African political ideas in *Return to the Source, Revolution in Guinea* and *The Weapon of Theory*. Cabral was assassinated by the Portuguese secret police (PIDE) in 1973.

Marvin ("Pancho") Camillo (1937-1988)

Marvin Camillo led theatrical workshops for inmates at the Sing Sing Correctional Facility at Ossining, N.Y. where he was responsible for encouraging then-inmate Miguel Piñero to write his Obie Award-winning play *Short Eyes*. At that time Camillo visited other prisons including the Bedford Hills Correctional Facility in Westchester County. His group at Bedford Hills evolved into *The Family*, a drama troupe which travelled to neighborhood venues throughout New York and eventually became the resident company of the Theater of the Riverside Church in Manhattan.

From the memorial program, Rosehill Cemetery, Linden, N.J.:

His interest and talent in the arts was expressed at a very early age. Visitors to his family's Brunswick Street (Newark, N.J.) residence could hear him singing in beautiful tones or see him drawing or practicing the latest mambo, cha-cha, or other dance routines with his many friends and relatives . . . In 1972 Marvin began his work with "The Family," a unique theater company founded by Marvin and created to assist ex-offenders, addicts, and disadvantaged youths in turning their lives around. As Marvin put it, "if you're involved in theater, there's no time for other things" . . . "The Family" took their fine performances all around the United States and abroad.

John Coltrane (1926-1967)

Trane, I always hooked up in my mind with Malcolm. I see them as similar kinds sweeping transformational forces. Coltrane was trying to get away from the tin pan alley jail—16/32 and the content and bone yard. Trane left behind the old and unliving forms in his historic playing with Gillespie, Charlie Parker and various other bands. When he began to use these innovative techniques, it caused a stir in the Black music world. It became harder to dismiss him as a kind of upstart. He was trying to get rid of the pop song chordal/scale and going into the free thing and using African and Indian rhythms. The energy that he used was also great. One tune would be the whole set, and go on for an hour. When he was playing like that, it was interesting and full of risk because he was continually experimenting and trying to find a new approach to the music.

Miles Davis (1926-1991)

All the people who came out of the so-called bop era were heroes to me from the beginning—Monk and Dizzy and Max Roach and Bird, all of them. I grew up with these people and celebrated them and came to understand the world through them. But along with Dizzy, Miles was one of my ultimate culture heroes. I loved the way he looked and dressed, the way he acted on the stage, and everything he did. When I was playing the trumpet I tried to sound like him.

I had a teacher who was trying to teach me that real full-toned "legit-imate" sound, but I wanted to get that Miles sound by trying to undo what the teacher wanted me to do. I tried to move the mouthpiece over to the side to get that kind of cracked sound. I had a little band for a minute before I went away to school. It served my purposes. That's pitiful because you ain't going to do anything with that.

Walter Davis, Jr. (1932-1990)

From the memorial program, St. Paul AME Church, East Orange, N.J.:

Pianist, arranger, and composer, Water Davis, Jr. performed with Dizzy Gillespie and Art Blakey and the Jazz Messengers as well as the Rolling Stones. He was a member of the East Orange, N.J. High School Class of 1951. After high school . . . he traveled to New York City where he played his first gig at the Apollo Bar on 125th Street . . . [and at this time] he studied classical music . . . and attended the Jul-liard School of Music . . . Walter's short lifetime was filled with his many accomplishments. He loved music; He loved his family; He loved life. He leaves to mourn his loss and cherish his memory . . . one son, four daughters, one brother, three aunts, nieces, nephews, cousins, and friends.

Owen Dodson (1914-1983)

As a playwright, poet, novelist, and teacher, Owen Dodson had a major influence on African-American theater. As a writer, Dodson was highly regarded. Twenty-seven of his thirty-seven plays and operas have been produced—two at the Kennedy Center. President Johnson invited him to the White House. He received Guggenheim, Rosenwald and Rockefeller Grants. His friends included Countee Cullen, W.H. Auden, Langston Hughes, Richard Wright, and Carl Van Vechten. He worked professionally with such actors as James Earl Jones, Sir John Gielgud and Sidney Poitier and brought Jean Anouilh's *Antigone* to 25,000 high school students and 25,000 adults in Watts, Los Angeles. He also made great contributions as a profes-sor of drama for 20 years at Howard University. In 20 years of teach-ing theater history, directing, and writing plays and criticism, his students included Debbie Allen, Richard Wesley, Charles Brown, and

Amiri Baraka. He was director of the premiere of James Baldwin's play *The Amen Corner*. Dodson's published works include the novels *Come Home Early, Child* and *Boy at the Window*, the poetry collections *Powerful Long Ladder* and *The Harlem Book of the Dead* (a book of photographs in collaboration with Camille Billops and James Van Der Zee), and the plays *Divine Comedy, Garden of Time*, and *Bayou Legend*.

John Birks "Dizzy" Gillespie (1917-1993)

Diz led an unusually orderly and healthy life as far as jazz lives go, which I attribute to his marriage to Lorraine (though he would be as fierce as you wanted when he was pushed too far). He also had a very playful way with words. For example, when I was interviewing him about Miles for an article once, I asked him to compare himself to Miles Davis. He said, "Miles is a great musician. He's always changing, always coming out with new ideas, but the biggest difference between me and Miles is that Miles makes way, way, way, way, way, way, way, way, way, way, way, way, way . . . more money . . . "

It was really ironic (and weird in a way) that I found myself delivering this eulogy. From my teens on, Diz was somebody I followed and even patterned myself after, in some ways. He was a great person, a very wise person, and one of my guardian spirits in terms of how you measure your own conduct.

James "Omar" Gray (1963-1990)

James ("Omar") Gray was raised in Newark. At the age of 12, the family moved their membership to New Hope Baptist Church where he served in the Inspirational Choir. He received his education in the Newark school system, graduating from West Side High School. He entered the U.S. Army upon graduation, training at Fort McClellan. He was murdered by some ignorant co-victim, when he tried to break up a fight.

From the memorial program, House of God, Orange N.J.:

James ("Omar") was a very affectionate person who left a great impact on everyone he met. He will be greatly missed by many. He leaves two daughters . . . two brothers . . . four sisters . . . a dearly beloved woman friend, and a host of nieces, nephews, and other relatives and friends.

Louise Gray (1971-1992)

Her life was ended before its time, like her brother before her. Adding to the bitterness of her death was the fact that their mother Rosa was a tireless community activist who struggled against the conditions that ultimately killed two of her children. As a young girl, Louise worked hard to finish high school even though she had a baby of her own. She died on a street corner in Irvington, N.J., a victim of a stabbing motivated by a confrontation between two groups.

Ellis B. Haizlip (1929-1991)

As the pioneering executive producer and television host of SOUL!, the Emmy Award-winning Public Broadcasting System (PBS) television series, Ellis Haizlip was widely recognized as a key figure in African-American arts and culture. Following his vision, SOUL! became a focal point for the dissemination of information during a time of black political and cultural emergence in the late '60s and early '70s, by bringing promising, emerging, and significant figures in African-American literature, dance, music, drama, and political activism to a national stage. Haizlip has also served as a theatrical producer, an arts administrator for New York State and New York City, and a consultant and board member to a number of cultural organizations, including the Alvin Ailey Dance Theater, the Gospel Music workshop of America, and the Bill T. Jones/Arne Zane Dance Company.

Specks Hicks (1933-1991)

Specs was an old friend of mine that I grew up with in Newark. He was the head of a big gang called "The Dukes," composed of boxers, that was the toughest gang in Newark in the early '50s. Specs was an addict and had the courage not only to clean himself up but start one of the first detox and rehab drug treatment programs in the U.S. His program was the first to originate with members of the local community. He found a way to use the resources that were available to him in the community and later got funding. He named it "Operation Coat Puller." (In other words I'm gonna pull your coat," he used to say.) Later we got to be friends and I always valued that friend-

ship. I always thought of him as a kind of role model; he taught me something valuable in the stance that he took toward the world—a cool summing up before taking any action, but then taking action when the moment required it.

Yusef Iman (1933-1984)

Yusef was primarily an actor, but also a poet and cultural activist and organizer, as well as a singer. He was perhaps the epitome of a Black Arts Movement artist. He was completely committed to the political ideals of the movement, particularly that of self-determination for African people. Yusef was an aggressively energetic person. To direct him was like trying to contain a storm. But he gave his most his utmost—his deepest, his best—because he was trying to make a revolution.

Tina Johnson-Landrum (1930-1995)

From the memorial program, Whigham Funeral Home, Newark, N.J.:

Her love for her children led her to become the PTA President at both Abington Avenue and Dr. William H. Horton Elementary Schools. As a community activist she served as a delegate for the National Black Convention, was a member of the CFUN Advisory Board, and also a board member for the "Little One" program. Through the '60s Tina fought for some of the rights and privileges that the citizens of this city now enjoy. She ran for the Board of Education on the "Save the Children" slate. She is well-known as a pioneer of Newark's "Old School." Her determination to educate children and make a difference led her to college at the age of 54 and she graduated from Bloomfield College of New Jersey with Cum Laude Honors and a Bachelor's Degree in Sociology. She received the Librarian of the Year Award. She worked at House of Prayer Day Care and Citadel of Hope Academy of Newark. She then taught for the Prestigious Chad School in Newark and one of her greatest pleasures was teaching [young children] to read.

"Philly" Joe Jones (1923-1985)

His real fame came with the Miles Davis group of the late '50s and early '60s. I knew him when he was playing with Miles. I would see him from time to time, but I only got to work with him a short time before he died, when Max Roach and Archie Shepp and I did a 3-hour improv at the Afro-American Museum in Philadelphia. Max said to me, "You can't come with no papers. We improvise so you improvise." The next time we were scheduled to do this at Columbia University, Max could not come, but Philly did and he was uncharacteristically deferential because, though he was a master musician, he felt like he was entering an area he didn't know as much about. He thought we were doing something important and he wanted to know if what he was doing was correct. He was a giant, but in this circumstance, he felt he was with someone who was going to make some overt political statement and was careful he didn't want to fuck it up.

Willie Jones (1929-1987)

He was a drummer and connoisseur of music. If you went to a club, you'd see Willie. He had a gig writing for a major music magazine from time to time. He was one of those guys that if you met him you knew you were going have a delightful conversation about something you were interested in.

Bob Kaufman (1925-1986)

Bob Kaufman was one of the founders of *Beatitude* magazine. He has been informally credited with inventing the term "beatnik." Kaufman was born in New Orleans, Louisiana and was one of 13 children of a German Orthodox Jewish father and a black Catholic mother from Martinique. Kaufman got his literary education in the U.S. Merchant Marine, which he joined when he was 13. In 20 years in the Merchant marine, Kaufman traveled around the world nine times, endured four shipwrecks, lost 40% of his hearing, and got a first-class, self-taught education in the classics of world literature. Kaufman was a jazz poet, dedicated to the spontaneous, oral tradition. As an advocate of political and social protest, he suffered imprisonment and was once given involuntary shock treatment. Beginning in 1963, he took a Buddhist vow of written and spoken silence which lasted for ten years to protest the Vietnam war. Among his best known works are the poem *Abomunist Manifesto* (1959) and the poetry collections *Solitudes Crowded with Loneliness* (1965, New Directions), *The Golden Sardine* (1967, City Lights), and *The Ancient Rain* (1981, New Directions).

Bob Kaufman was the prototypical beatnik before beatnik got coined. He never got the ink that a lot of them did. I first got wind of him in those Beatitudes *that he published on the West Coast. He was the first guy to use that proto-beat jargon. I think Bob is actually one of the sources of the modern kind of American surreal imagery— Native American—rather than imported from Europe. He was a homegrown surrealist and one of the earliest anarcho-poet types. In other words, a lot of beat mystique that had to do with the mind-change or mind-out, I first got from Bob. He had a completely developed surreal look at America.*

William Kunstler (1919-1995)

Among attorney William Kunstler's clients were Dr. Martin Luther King, Jr., Adam Clayton Powell, inmates charged with rebellion in the 1971 Attica prison uprising, the Chicago Seven (Jerry Rubin, Tom Hayden, Rennie Davis, David Dellinger, Abbie Hoffman, John R. Froines, and Lee Weiner), Stokley Carmichael, Bobby Seale, Wayne Williams (convicted of the "Atlanta Child Murders" in the '80s), Darryl Cabey (one of the youths shot by subway gunman Bernhard Goetz) in New York City, and El Sayyid Nosair, the alleged assassin of Rabbi Meir Kahane. At the time of his death, he was contributing to the defense of a suspect in the 1993 bombing of the World Trade Center.

He was a stand-up guy, someone you could depend on, a soldier in the movement. He was there and he had his own ideology that was resistance. I called him the law artist, Der Kunstler. Bill was a person I could use as a kind of model for a multinational revolutionary party. If you only come in contact with racists or people in the establishment who have the standard kind of American line you think that you can't have any unity with them in the struggle because they think the system is all right. When you find someone who was willing to

say something and fight in some real way then it encouraged you
about the movement itself.

Joseph S. ("Smiley") Landrum (1935-1989)

From the memorial program, Whigham Funeral Home Chapel, Newark, N.J.:

The primary remembrance we all have of "Smiley" is his love of life and his deep and committed love of his wife and companion Tina " [Johnson-Landrum] and their three generations of children . . . Joe cared deeply for his fellow workers at the Post Office and the Newark School Board, both places where he worked for many years. Joe strived hard to help solve union problems and make conditions better for all. He also looked after the schoolchildren he attended to on his school bus with as much love and care as if they were his own . . . .

Malcolm X (1925-1965)

*Malcolm was the most decisive political influence on my life. His emergence served as a catalyst to change my whole view of the world. I wasn't close to that Nation of Islam stuff but when Malcolm became the maximum black revolutionary leader—I criticized King for that non-violent integrationist thing. When they blew up King's house after he helped lead the Montgomery bus boycott people came with guns held over their heads saying, "Dr. King what should we do?" He said, "If any blood be shed, let it be our blood." **That** was when he was elevated to "Our Leader." I couldn't stand that non-violence resistance. You needed to be talking about those damn sheriffs taking seminars on nonviolence, not our people. When Malcolm was talking about self-reliance and self-defense for our whole generation that was a revelation. His ideas made me reevaluate what I should be doing with my life.*

Bob Marley (1945-1981)

"Won't you help me sing these songs of redemption, they're all I've ever had, redemption song."

—Bob Marley, *Redemption Song*

Kasisi Sadikifu Nakawa (Paul Arnold Sanders) (1945-1988)

From the memorial program, Robeson Campus Center, Rutgers University, Newark, N.J.:

Paul was an organizer and a fighter who consistently upheld the right to self-determination for all people. When the liberation movements of the African continent reached out for support from the African-American brothers and sisters, Paul was there for the founding of the African Liberation Support Committee (ALSC) . . . He was a man ahead of his time in many ways. Seeing the need for an improvement in the quality of life for his people within the confines of the existing system, Paul was a member of the Committee for a Unified Newark, and was instrumental in the work to elect Ken Gibson, the first Black mayor of a major Northeastern city. Paul helped organize the National Black Political Assembly—the body which many historians view as the predecessor of the Rainbow Coalition . . . His work with students spanned three decades. This work included: leading [and winning] the struggle at Rutgers-Newark to name the student center after fallen freedom-fighter Paul Robeson in the '60s; protesting police killings of Black youth in the '70s; organizing parents, educators and workers for an elected school board; and support work for the liberation movements of Southern Africa in the '80s.

Larry Neal (1937-1981)

Poet, essayist, playwright, folklorist, filmmaker, editor, and teacher, Larry Neal was one of the most important figures in the Black Arts Movement. In addition to being (with Amiri Baraka) cofounder of the Black Arts organization in Harlem and coeditor of *Black Fire*, an anthology of Black Arts Movement writings, he served as education director of the New York Panther Party. Later he directed the Commission on the Arts and Humanities in Washington, D.C., and taught at the City College of New York and at Yale and Howard Universities.

Okot p'Bitek (1931-1982)

Ugandan poet Okot p'Bitek achieved an international reputation as a major African literary voice with the publication of *Song of Lawino* in 1966. In this unprecedentedly original work, p'Bitek drew on

Acoli and Lango traditional songs of praise, abuse, joy, humor, sorrow, sympathy, and satire, using storytelling and conventions of oral art to invent a new literary genre free of European reference and technique. Other major poems p'Bitek published include *Song of Ocol* (1970) and *Song of Prisoner/Song of Malaya* (published as *Two Songs* in 1971). Throughout a busy academic and professional career, he wrote scholarly works, essays on literature, philosophy, religion, politics, history, sex, and pop music.

He wrote traditional epic poetry. While it looks like an African Ballad, it is also a non-traditional Okot form. His message was the picture of what total submission to evil does to you, how the people had to submit to this weakness and evil and how it affected them personally. His works sum up a whole period of post-colonial transition with the political and psychological hangovers that come with all that. To wit: "How Africans reject everything African having been exposed to European colonialism."

Being an independent voice, Brother Okot was always a hop skip and jump from getting wiped. What saved him was that he was famous as a great traditional dancer. He had enough stature as a dancer that they wouldn't kill him. Okot had the celebrity, as a dancer, in Uganda, that, say, Fred Astaire had in the U.S., and that meant that they could make his life difficult, but they couldn't do all the things to him they had in mind. He was still Okot the dancer as well as Okot the poet (which they hated). I got to know him near the end on a trip to Rome with my wife Amina and poet Jayne Cortez, but he was very haunted and run down and was doing himself in by that time.

Miguel Piñero (1946-1988)

As a playwright, poet, and actor, Miguel Piñero brought keen-eyed humanity to the themes of prison life, drug dealing, hustling, and the realities of life in the urban underclass. He began writing in prison, and his first play, *Short Eyes: The Killing of a Sex Offender by the Inmates of the House of Detention Awaiting Trial* (1974) received Obie and New York Drama Critics Awards. He also wrote *Eulogy for a Small Time Thief* (1977), *The Sun Always Shines for the Cool* (1978), and *A Midnight Moon at the Greasy Spoon* (1981). As an actor he appeared in a number of films including the movie adaptation of *Short Eyes* (1977) and *Fort Apache, The Bronx* (1981), and on several network police dramas such as *Baretta* and *Miami Vice*. At the time when *Short Eyes* was produced, he opened up his East 10 Street Apartment as a theater and poetry workshop for young people to "instill pride and confidence in their own intelligence." This workshop was the birthplace of the New York based "NuYorican" poetry movement of Puerto Rican poets. With Miguel Algarin, he edited *NuYorican Poets: An Anthology of Puerto Rican Words and Feelings* (1975, Morrow).

Keeping Mikey cool was an industry. He was hooked up on the kind of street life—the drugs and all kinds of other wild excesses. He was always in and out of jail, thrown out of his crib and in the street. But he was a fine and important writer and his work was an insistent assertion of the aliveness of even the rejected. Short Eyes *was an eye-opener. He was trying to show that the prison has its order and morality and a prison culture. Mikey was the ultimate New York Puerto Rican. He was one of Puerto Rico's sons, but what he was doing had to do with what was unique to being a Puerto Rican in New York.*

Don Gabriel Pullen (1941-1995)

He was one of the musicians that came up to the Black Arts [Repertory Theater] in the early days. When he was coming up, he played with Charlie Mingus and other groups. Ultimately, Don was more known for his kind of instrumental brilliance and innovation. You could link him with Cecil Taylor in a way but with a little more bluesey funky approach. He was a good friend of mine and I still play his music almost every night.

Sun Ra (1914?-1993)

With his band, the Arkestra, pianist and bandleader Sun Ra created amazing musical spectacles that included drum choirs, orchestral Bebop, singers, dancers, acrobats, films, light shows, Egyptian/outer space surrealism, camp, pandemonium, and spirituality. He began his career as a jazz sideman with such figures as Coleman Hawkins, Stuff Smith, and Fletcher Henderson.

In the '50s he began an experimental jazz band that was the forerunner of the Arkestra. In the late '60s, he moved to Philadelphia and he and his band lived in a cooperative situation through the end of his life. Despite his flamboyance (he insisted that he was born on Saturn and that musicians were extinct on this planet, their place taken by actors with instruments), he helped lead a revival of interest in traditional jazz heritage and was able to survive commercially without pandering to the fashion of the day.

I got to meet him close up when he'd come uptown to talk at the Black Arts. He'd come there to talk to people for eight hours at a time. He was a serious investigator of all these kinds of metaphysical things. He was also a great analyst of language. Some of the things I do now in terms of puns and picking the language apart to show its origin in its essence past what you think it means, I got that from him, that was Sun Ra's kick.

Charlie James Richardson (1928-1993)

He was my father-in-law. We respected each other, the Marxist and the Advanced Worker. He lived the last 13 years in a motorized wheelchair without complaint. Check that. He got a big settlement after his accident. It was the union people who got him the money. He was able to live comfortably and continue to be the center and foundation of his part of the family.

From the memorial program, Emmanuel Church of Christ DOC, Newark, N.J.:

At the age of 18, Charlie joined the Army. There he began his legacy of being behind the wheel of anything that could be driven. In the Army, he operated a bulldozer in the construction of airstrips and road construction, a M-2 crane and other heavy equipment. In 1951 . . . he moved to Newark . . . Initially "Big Charlie" was employed as a truck driver for various trucking companies . . . In 1981 [he] had a trucking accident that paralyzed him and left him a quadri-plegic . . . Flat on his back, Big Charlie added another six feet to his stature . . . Big Charlie was much more than a big man in stature. His heart was much bigger than he was. He always had a word of encouragement for whomever came to him . . . No problem was too big or too hard that he didn't take on, and take care of. A people man, a father and a friend. Charlie joined the Emmanuel Church of Christ DOC in April 1990, where he attended church functions and other affairs in his wheelchair. When his daughter opened the New Life Evangelistic Ministry in 1992, he was a founding trustee.

Anna Russ (1885-1962) and Fanny Jones (1885-1976)

I love them both very much. My Grandmother Russ seemed like the sweetest and most loving most spiritual person I ever met. She could pinch you until your nose fell off, if you were making noise in church, but you knew you deserved it and you were going to get that anyway. My Grandmother Jones, who lived in South Carolina, seemed like a very wise and calm and judicious person.

G.L. ("George") Russ (1902-1983)

From *The Autobiography of LeRoi Jones/Amiri Baraka*, (1984, Freundlich Books):

My uncle was the exotic personality in our house—on the road, and when he came home, in checked sports coats. He was a man-about-town, like they say. . . [His] railroad job let him travel and gave him that air of urbanity and sophistication. He had a porkpie hat he wore sometimes with the snap brim down. He went to New York and did his shopping and spent a lot of time over there. Plus he thought up a scam that seemed like a hip idea the more I got to understand it. G.L. sold the sandwiches on the Pullman, those flat, dry sandwiches the railroad sold. But G.L. figured that he could sell some sandwiches too, for G.L., since it was free enterprise and what not. So he had my grandmother (and we helped too) make spiced ham sandwiches with cheese and mayonnaise, modest but colored good. The whole kitchen table would be laid out with "G.L.'s sandwiches." My grandmother turned it into a real cottage industry, and it was the focus of many family discussions.

Al Ryan (1931-1980)

He was a lawyer in Los Angeles. In the '60s he got involved in the black liberation movement in an organic way. He was part of the National Black Political Convention in Gary, Indiana in 1972. He was one of the organizers of the Los Angeles Black Assembly. He was the convener of the Los Angeles assembly. Whenever I went to L.A. I'd see him. He was one of my best friends. Just before he died he set my wife and kids and I up in a cottage in Venice Beach for our visit. Al was a guy on the scene. I went to his house one time and there in his living room were Muhammad Ali, Kareem Abdul-Jabbar, and Jim Brown. Because he was a lawyer he had a kind of reserve about him but also a sweet person, and one with a deep sense of responsibility. A lot of the legal work he did was pro bono. He was very dedicated to the principal of black self-determination.

Michael Smith (1954-1983)

He was a Dub poet, who wrote in what the Jamaicans call "Nation Language"—the voice of the working class Jamaicans. Dub is a poetry that uses reggae rhythms with natural spoken language. I became aware of his work through the Dub poet Linton Kwesi Johnson and Darcus How's magazine Race Today. *His best known works are the records* It a Come *[also published by City Lights] and* Mi Cyaan Believe It *(Me Can't Believe It). Mikey Smith was murdered in Kingston outside the Jamaican Labour Party headquarters by people associated with the Seaga administration. Mikey had insulted a minister at a public forum by asking an inconvenient question and the next night he was stoned to death—like in the bible. When he died, I went to Brixton [a largely Anglo-Caribbean section of London] to speak and give a eulogy.*

Al White (1937-1984) and Tom White (1935-1984)

Tom White, his brother Al and their father, all died in the same year. Tom was a businessman and in the '60s the whole question of black-owned business developing in an independent way and having goods from Africa was considered very progressive. He had the store to sell African goods in Newark and this was celebrated by us. At the time, there were no stores that specialized in African goods from the conti-

nent. The store was called Worldwide and it had things not just from Africa but literally from all over. We rallied to him. It wasn't being done by Macy's or Kresge's or Bamberger's but one of us. He tried to be a progressive influence, as well as a businessman. The business came out of his feeling and commitment to the community.

Art Williams (1922-1980)

He ran a club called, "The Cellar." During its time it was the most important spot for music in Newark. It was the one that had the people; there were bigger ones and more advertised ones but this was the key one for jazz. People like Albert Ayler, Marion Brown, and Hank Mobley and his group played there. I used to read there. It would draw audiences from New York because these were world-known musicians. Art ran this club right up until the end of his life.

Harold "Mhisani" Wilson (1934-1980)

One of the founders of the United Brothers and the Committee for a Unified Newark. He also led the organizing and campaigning which resulted in the election of Newark's first black mayor.

About the Author

Amiri Baraka (LeRoi Jones) was born in Newark, New Jersey, in 1934. He attended Rutgers and Howard Universities, leaving the latter in 1954 to enlist in the U.S. Air Force. In 1957, he settled in New York's Greenwich Village and became a central figure in the bohemian scene, collaborating on and coediting several important literary publications, including *Yugen, Floating Bear,* and *Kulchur.* He gained national attention in 1964, with the New York production of his Obie Award-winning play, *Dutchman.* After the death of Malcolm X in 1965, Baraka became a Black Nationalist, moving first to Harlem and then back to Newark. In 1974, he proclaimed his commitment to International Socialism, Third World Marxism, and definitively repudiated nationalism.

Baraka has produced over twenty plays, three jazz operas, seven non-fiction books, a novel, and some fifteen volumes of poetry. He has been the recipient of grants from both the Rockefeller Foundation and the National Endowment of the Arts, as well as the Langston Hughes Award from the City College of New York. He is currently a professor of Africana Studies at SUNY-Stony Brook. He lives with his wife, the poet Amina Baraka, in Newark.